Carlo Edwards

LAWRENCE TIBBETT AS THE EMPEROR JONES
AS PRESENTED AT THE METROPOLITAN OPERA HOUSE

Please Mother! I'd rather
do it myself!

Noble's Comparative Classics

MACBETH
William Shakespeare

THE EMPEROR JONES
Eugene O'Neill

Edited By

BENJAMIN A. HEYDRICK, M. A.

AND

ALFRED A. MAY, M. A.

NOBLE AND NOBLE, *Publishers, Inc.*

67 IRVING PLACE   NEW YORK CITY

THE COMPARATIVE CLASSICS

IN recognition of the demand for more modern literature and in the belief that a study of the Classics is greatly enhanced by comparison, the publishers have launched a new series, *The Comparative Classics* based upon a new idea: that of presenting an older classic side by side with a modern one of the same type. This plan has several advantages. There has been a strong demand for more modern literature in secondary courses; there is at the same time a feeling that no English education is complete without some knowledge of the great classics. The present plan meets both demands. Furthermore, it is generally recognized that one of the most fruitful ways of studying literature is by the comparative method. To place side by side two plays, two poems or two essays in which the same theme is treated by different writers makes clear at once the characteristics of the two authors. It also affords a means of studying the larger aspects of the two works, of comparing them in theme and treatment, rather than concentrating upon the text of one. It is the practice of many teachers, after studying a classic, to assign as supplementary reading a modern book of the same type. Here both books are conveniently placed within a single cover.

Noble's Comparative Classics

MACBETH—THE EMPEROR JONES

ROBINSON CRUSOE—THE RAFT—THE ANCIENT MARINER

SILAS MARNER—THE PEARL

JULIUS CAESAR—ELIZABETH THE QUEEN

ROMEO AND JULIET—CYRANO DE BERGERAC

IDYLLS OF THE KING—THE KING'S HENCHMAN

HAMLET—ELECTRA—BEYOND THE HORIZON

COMPARATIVE ESSAYS—PRESENT AND PAST

COMPARATIVE COMEDIES—PRESENT AND PAST

(She Stoops to Conquer, The Rivals, Holiday, Goose Hangs High)

CONTENTS

Contents

INTRODUCTION

BIOGRAPHICAL NOTES

IF you should ever go to England, of course you would make a pilgrimage out to that pleasant, central county of Warwick, which enshrines the little town of Stratford-on-Avon. So many thousands every year do make that pilgrimage that the thrifty inhabitants have turned the whole place into a veritable Shakespeare museum. All available documents and mementos have been collected in one or another of the spots associated with his life, so that as you go from place to place, the whole story lies open before you.

The beginning and the end are in Trinity Church, the ancient, familiar building by the river. Here the Parish Register stands open at two important pages. On one, a line of cramped writing, under the date of April 26, 1564, announces in Latin the christening of William, son of John Shakespeare. There is no known record of his birth, but, as children were usually christened when three days old and as, moreover, there is a persistent tradition that he died on his birthday, the date April 23 is commonly accepted. A few pages farther on in the same book, under the date April 25, 1616, appears the burial entry of *Will Shakespeare, Gent.* Between these two records lie the fifty-two years so vital to the history of English literature.

I

The double house on Henley Street, where the poet was born, is carefully preserved as the most precious of all the museums. The birth chamber is a small, bare, low-ceiled room, the walls of which are closely scribbled with the autographs of the great and the obscure who have done homage here. The living-room has an interesting ingle-nook, from which, through the wide chimney-top, one may catch glimpses of the sky. It is easy to imagine the boy Shakespeare sitting here and thinking "long, long thoughts." In a small garden behind the house, grow specimens of all the flowers mentioned in the plays. Recalling the many famous flower passages, one realizes the ambitious nature of this project.

The other side of the house is said to have been used by John Shakespeare in his business. Just what that was seems doubtful. He is spoken of as farmer, glover, wool trader. He appears to have been a merchant of some sort and to have been in prosperous circumstances when his son was born. Various documents on exhibition attest his success and the esteem of his townsmen. He held several offices, among them that of High Bailiff, the equivalent of Mayor. Though there are, here, few records of the poet's mother, Mary Arden, it is known that she came of an old and substantial Warwickshire family and brought her husband considerable landed property.

Not far from Henley Street, the grammar school which Shakespeare attended is still in active service. Between a modern chapel and a picturesque row of old almshouses,

SHAKESPEARE'S BIRTHPLACE

Bunny Hutch, Stratford

ANNE HATHAWAY'S COTTAGE

through an inconspicuous gateway, one enters an inner court-yard and climbs a staircase to the quaint, oak-timbered class-rooms. Here, for perhaps seven years of his life, the boy recited his Latin verbs, and acquired what other learning the place had to offer. The bench at which he sat has now been removed to the house on Henley Street; but an inscription, suspiciously near the master's desk, marks the place he oc-cupied. At fourteen he is said to have left school. Perhaps he was needed at home, as documents show that John Shake-speare's affairs were not going well. About this time he was sued for debt, and later he was deprived of his alderman's gown.

The next four years of the young poet's life have left few traces. Of course if you choose to believe the tradition that he was caught stealing deer and was severely reprimanded by the owner, Sir Thomas Lucy, you may make a brief ex-pedition out to Charlecote, the Lucy estate. There you may see the stately house, the park with the deer still placidly feeding, and the tumble-down stile where a fleeing culprit might be caught. But probably deer were not kept in the park in Shakespeare's time and the whole story rests on such a flimsy foundation that it is better rejected.

You will, however want to walk across the fields to Shot-tery, following Shakespeare's footsteps to the thatched roof cottage where lived Anne Hathaway. It is an interesting place, furnished more completely than the Stratford house, with furniture that is of the period if not actually original. Here, perhaps on this very oaken settle by the fire, the young couple carried on their courtship. They were married in 1582, when the youthful bridegroom was only eighteen and his bride twenty-six.

Whether or not this marriage was happy is in dispute. Certain references and the fact that he lived in London without her have been taken as hints that all was not well. But the evidence is inconclusive. There was every reason why he should go to London and should go alone. By the time he was twenty-one he had three children to support, a daughter Susanna and the twins, Judith and Hamnet. There was little gainful occupation for a young man in so small a town, and, if he intended to make his way in the city, it would be far cheaper and easier to provide for his family at home. Ample proof exists that he made frequent trips to Stratford during his London period and when he had amassed enough money we know that he returned there to end his days with his wife and children.

Of that most important twenty years in London, Stratford has naturally few direct records; but the results of his stay there are visible in the early editions of his plays preserved in the Henley Street museum. Little indeed is known of the steps by which Shakespeare rose to eminence in the theater. He may have served first in some humble capacity; then gained a place on the stage as actor; later, revised or adapted plays; and finally gained enough experience and skill to produce, in his own right, those marvelous works that have never since been equaled by any writer. He was associated with the theater also in a business way, as, at his death, he owned part interests in both the Blackfriars and the Globe playhouses.

In 1597 he purchased New Place, the finest estate in Stratford, as a final home. Not a vestige of this house remains. Only the site is left and a garden of later date. Even the famous mulberry tree which Shakespeare is said to have planted was cut down by a peevish owner who was troubled by the questions of literary pilgrims. But reports describe it as a beautiful place, and here Shakespeare spent some years before his death. His son Hamnet had died years before and his daughter Susanna had married Dr. John Hall of the town; but Judith and Anne remained and old friends and associates surrounded him. He died here April 23, 1616.

We must go back to the village church to see his grave. He is buried within the church, just inside the chancel rail. A plain flat stone guards his resting-place with the warning *Curst be he that moves my bones.* Beside him lie his wife, his daughter Susanna and her husband, Dr. Hall. On the wall above his grave is a bust in colors, said to be an authentic likeness.

Many contemporary references indicate the place that Shakespeare held in his lifetime. Greene speaks of him with envy, Jonson with affection and admiration. Meres gives a list of his plays. He is mentioned first among the actors who walked in procession at the coronation of James I. He died, prosperous and honored. But probably, for all his wonderful imagination, never in its wildest flights did he dream that, more than three hundred years after his death, his plays would still be acted not only in his own country but in far distant lands, and that every year thousands of visitors from across the sea would walk the streets of his native town, seeking out and treasuring every relic of his sojourn there. Yet so it is. All nations and lands pay tribute to this man, for he spoke a universal language

"With tears and laughter for all time."

SHAKESPEARE'S WORKS

The plays, considered chronologically, fall naturally into four main divisions, each marking a distinct advance over the preceding in mastery of technique, in beauty and variety of expression, and in depth of spiritual experience. Professor Dowden has gone so far as to give names to these periods, showing his conception of this advance.

He calls the first *In the workshop,* because, as he says, the author was still "learning his trade as a dramatic craftsman." The second he names *In the world,* for it was now that the poet "came to understand the world and the men in it; his plays began to deal in an original and powerful way with the matter of history." *Out of the depths* is the third period when Shakespeare had known sorrow and had begun "to sound with his imagination the depths of the human heart; to inquire into the darkest and saddest parts of human life; to study the great mystery of evil." The last division is *On the heights* because now the poet had learned the secret of life and had "ascended out of the turmoil and trouble of action, out of the darkness and tragic mystery,—to a pure and serene elevation."

The chief plays are as follows: The dates are approximate.

PERIOD I

1590-1594

Love's Labor Lost
Comedy of Errors
Midsummer Night's Dream
Two Gentlemen of Verona
Richard III
Romeo and Juliet

PERIOD II

1594-1600

King John
Merchant of Venice
Henry IV—Parts I and II
Henry V
Merry Wives of Windsor
Much Ado About Nothing
Taming of the Shrew
As You Like It
Twelfth Night
All's Well That Ends Well

PERIOD III

1600-1609

Hamlet
Julius Cæsar
Measure for Measure
Othello
Macbeth
King Lear
Antony and Cleopatra
Coriolanus

PERIOD IV

1609-1612

Cymbeline
The Tempest
The Winter's Tale

Poetry

Venus and Adonis—*1593*
Rape of Lucrece—*1594*
Sonnets—*1609*

PUBLICATION

During Shakespeare's lifetime, there was no authorized edition of his works. Indeed efforts were made to keep them out of print. They were intended to be seen on the stage, not read. If they should appear in book form, rival companies might, because of the lack of copyright laws, produce them and reap the financial reward. Only the actors' prompt books and a few, small, usually pirated copies, called quartos, existed.

But about seven years after the author's death, two of his friends, John Heminge and Henry Condell, made a conscientious effort to present an authorized edition, using the original manuscripts and some of the quartos. This was the famous First Folio of 1623.

PLOT STRUCTURE

Drama implies struggle. The uneventful life, pursuing the even tenor of its way without serious ups or downs, may be happy but it is not dramatic. Such a life might be graphically represented by a straight line. Nothing happens and we leave the hero just where we found him, older perhaps, but otherwise unchanged.

But suppose something does happen. An inciting force of some kind drives this complacent person to action. He tries to gain an end and is met with opposition. He fights against a rival, or against his own nature, or against fate. Drama is present at once, and his line of life shows a steady rise in interest.

Presently affairs reach a crisis. A decisive step settles his future fortunes. Its importance may not be immediately apparent, but it is a turning point in his fate and his success or failure is now inevitable. The action falls.

Finally the end of the adventure is reached. He has succeeded and the ending is happy, or he has failed and we have tragedy, perhaps death. At any rate, his life has been dramatic.

In recognition of this principle, Shakespearean drama was divided always into five acts. The first explained the situation of the hero and introduced the complication that was to stir him from his even path. The second act increased difficulties, tying the action securely into a knot. Act Three rose to a turning point and began the falling action. The fourth act resolved the difficulties, and the fifth provided the catastrophe or the happy outcome. Often just before the end there was a moment of suspense when the hero's fate hung in the balance. But the turning point was always a sure guide. As it pointed toward success or failure, so must the ending be.

This division is often graphically represented thus:

ACT III—CRISIS

ACT II
COMPLICATION

ACT IV
RESOLUTION

ACT I
INTRODUCTION

ACT V
OUTCOME

For this reason, one who wishes to understand a Shakespearean play must discover first what is the task to be attempted and what are the clashing interests. Next, he must watch each act to learn what definite step in the progress of the play is made; he must decide what is the turning point and where it occurs; he must trace the falling action and note the outcome. Only so may he appreciate the full dramatic import.

One convention, generally ignored by Shakespeare, but carefully observed by many of his contemporaries, is known as that of the three unities. The unity of time provided that the action of the play should cover no more than twenty-four hours. Unity of place made all action occur in one spot. Whatever could not so occur must be related by messengers. Unity of action forbade the introduction of more than one main plot or focus of interest. As the first two greatly limited the playwright's scope, we are grateful to Shakespeare for disregarding them. The third, evidently, is still in force.

Modern drama has changed principally in the matter of simplification and shortening. It still recognizes the necessity of contending interests. Without struggle, there is no play. The old outline of introduction, complication, crisis, resolution, outcome, is still followed. But it is a bit more casual; the edges are not quite so clean-cut. Sometimes it is difficult to follow. Moreover the action has been condensed. Acts I and II have been combined, as have Acts IV and V. A modern play of more than three acts is rare, and often there are but two or even one.

Many of the old stage conventions have disappeared. The first two of the unities are entirely outmoded. Long speeches, so dear to the Elizabethan, do not suit the modern taste. The soliloquy and the aside, which were such convenient ways of showing the actor's inmost thought, are seldom used. But the essential element of conflict is unchanged.

An interesting comparison may be made by noting carefully the development of plot in the two plays presented. Questions at the back of the book are intended to direct attention to certain phases of this discussion.

SOURCES OF MACBETH

In nearly all of his plays, Shakespeare took the plot or story from some other book. For example, the play *Julius Cæsar* was based upon the lives of Cæsar and Brutus as given in Plutarch's *Lives of Illustrious Greeks and Romans*. The plot of *Macbeth* he found in an old history, *Chronicles of Scotland*, by Ralph Holinshed. An extract from this will give an idea of the book; the passage chosen describes the first meeting of Macbeth with the witches.

"Shortly after happened a strange and uncouth wonder, which afterward was the cause of much trouble in the land of Scotland, as ye shall after hear. It fortuned as Macbeth and Banquo journeyed toward Forres, where the king as then lay, they went sporting by the way together without other company, save only themselves, passing through the woods and fields, when suddenly in the midst of a laund there met them three women in strange and ferly apparel, resembling creatures of an elder world, whom when they attentively beheld, wondering much at the sight, the first of them spake and said: 'All hail, Macbeth, Thane of Glamis!' (for he had lately entered into that dignity and office by the death of his father Sinel). The second of them said: 'All hail, Macbeth, that hereafter shall be King of Scotland!'

"Then Banquo: 'What manner of women,' saith he, 'are you, that seem so little favorable unto me, where as to my fellow here, besides high offices, ye assign also the kingdom, appointing forth nothing for me at all?' 'Yes,' saith the first of them, 'we promise greater benefits unto thee than unto him; for he shall reign indeed but with an unlucky end; neither shall he leave any issue behind him to succeed in his place, where contrarily thou indeed shalt not reign at all, but of thee those shall be born which shall govern the Scottish kingdom by long order of continual descent.' Herewith the foresaid women vanished immediately out of their sight. This was reputed at the first but some vain fantastical illusion by Macbeth and Banquo, insomuch that Banquo would call Macbeth in jest, King of Scotland; and Macbeth again would call him in sport likewise the father of many kings. But afterward the common opinion was, that these women were either the weird sisters, that is, as ye would say, the goddesses of destiny, or else some nymphs or fairies, endued with knowledge of prophecy by their necromantical science, because everything came to pass as they had spoken.

"For shortly after, the Thane of Cawdor being condemned at Forres of treason against the king committed, his lands, livings, and offices were given of the king's liberality to Macbeth. The same night after, at supper, Banquo jested with him and said: 'Now Macbeth thou hast obtained those things which the two former sisters prophesied, there remaineth only for thee to purchase that which the third said should come to pass.' Whereupon Macbeth revolving the thing in his mind.

began even then to devise how he might attain to the king-dom; but yet he thought with himself that he must tarry a time, which should advance him thereto, by the divine provi-dence, as it had come to pass in his former preferment."

This shows that Shakespeare followed Holinshed rather closely in this place. But in other places he departed widely from the source. The account of the murder of Duncan is very different. In Holinshed, Banquo knows of the intended murder, and promises to aid Macbeth. The murder is performed by four of Macbeth's servants, instead of by Macbeth. Further, we are told in Holinshed that Macbeth after gaining the crown, ruled for ten years very justly, and put down many evils in the land. But afterwards he showed himself hostile to Banquo, and caused his death as told in the play. After this he began to oppress his people, so that they were in fear of their lives. He began a great castle, called Dunsinane, and forced all his nobles to come with their followers and work upon it. Macduff sent workmen, but declined to come him-self, and this refusal angered Macbeth. We quote from Holinshed again:

"Neither could he afterward abide to look upon the said Macduff, either for that he thought his puissance over-great, either else for that he had learned of certain wizards, in whose words he put great confidence, for that the prophecy had happened so right which the three fairies or weird sisters had declared unto him, how that he ought to take heed of Macduff, who in time to come should seek to destroy him.

"And surely hereupon had he put Macduff to death, but that a certain witch, whom he had in great trust, had told him that he never should be slain with man born of any woman, nor vanquished till the wood of Birnam came to the castle of Dunsinane.

"By this prophecy Macbeth put all fear out of his heart, supposing he might do what he would, without any fear to be punished for the same, for by the one prophecy he believed it was impossible for any man to vanquish him, and by the other impossible to slay him. This vain hope caused him to do many outrageous things, to the grievous oppression of his subjects."

Note how much Shakespeare has added to this, having the apparitions arise and make the predictions, and having the show of eight kings appear.

Holinshed tells, but very briefly, that Macbeth attacked the castle of Macduff and caused his wife and children to be slain. The interview between Malcolm and Macduff in England follows Holinshed closely. The incident of cutting down the boughs at Birnam Wood, and the fight between Macduff and Macbeth are also in Holinshed.

From this it is evident that Shakespeare followed Holinshed for the main incidents of the story, though he made changes freely. But there are important parts of the play for which Holinshed gave no suggestion whatever. The banquet scene, where the ghost of Banquo appears, is entirely Shakespeare's invention. The famous sleep-walking scene, too, is all Shakespeare's. The letter written by Macbeth, and Lady Macbeth's comments upon it, the scene where Macbeth imagines he sees the dagger, the Porter scene, the witches brewing their hellbroth—all these are Shakespeare's invention.

And of course, the language of the play is Shakespeare's, not Holinshed's. When Macbeth says

> "Tomorrow and tomorrow and tomorrow
> Creeps in this petty pace from day to day,
> And all our yesterdays have lighted fools
> The way to dusty death. Out, out brief candle,
> Life's but a walking shadow, a poor player
> That struts and frets his hour upon the stage
> And then is heard no more."

This, and the other famous passages in the play are the words of the poet, not of the historian.

To conclude, then, Shakespeare took an old story, changed it to suit his purposes, invented other incidents, and told the whole in his own matchless language.

VERSIFICATION

THIS play, like all of Shakespeare's, is written in blank verse. This is a form of poetry without rhyme; it differs from prose in that all the lines contain the same number of syllables, and that these syllables are so arranged that every other one is accented. For example, take the line

"I think our country sinks beneath the yoke."

If you read it aloud, you will see that the syllables *think, coun, sinks, neath, yoke* are accented, the others are light, or unaccented. If we mark the accented syllables thus ━, and the unaccented thus ◡, we have a pattern like this for the whole line:

◡ ━ ◡ ━ ◡ ━ ◡ ━ ◡ ━

You note that the marks may be separated into groups, like this:

◡ ━   ◡ ━   ◡ ━   ◡ ━   ◡ ━

Each of these groups of two syllables is called a foot, and this particular foot, made up of an unaccented syllable followed by an accented syllable, is called iambic. There are five of these feet in a line; a line of five feet is called a pentameter line. Hence to describe the line in terms of meter, we would call it iambic pentameter.

But it would be a mistake to suppose that all the lines in the play follow this regular pattern. Take the very next line:

"It weeps, it bleeds, and each new day a gash,"

In reading that aloud, one would accent the words *weeps, bleeds, each, new, day, gash.* That would give you a pattern like this:

⏑ — ⏑ — ⏑ — — — ⏑ —

You see that the words *new day* form a foot in which both syllables are accented, — —. This is called a spondaic foot.

Take another line:

⏑ — ⏑ — ⏑ ⏑ ⏑ — ⏑ —

"There's no thing serious in mor tal ity."

Here the word *in* and the first syllable of *mortality* are both light, or unaccented, making what is called a pyrrhic foot, thus ⏑ ⏑.

And the following line is still different:

— ⏑ ⏑ — ⏑ — ⏑ — ⏑ —

"All is but toys; renown and grace is dead."

Here the first foot is made up of an accented syllable followed by an unaccented one, — ⏑. This is called a trochaic foot.

Let us now take a passage of several consecutive lines, and mark the accented and unaccented syllables.

⏑ — ⏑ — ⏑ — ⏑ — ⏑ ⏑
1. "Is this a dagger that I see before me

⏑ — ⏑ — ⏑ — ⏑ — ⏑ — ⏑
2. The handle towards my hand? Come, let me clutch thee

⏑ — ⏑ — ⏑ — ⏑ — ⏑ —
3. I have thee not, and yet I see thee still.

     ‒ �’   ‒   ‒ ˘ ‒ ˘   ‒ ˘ ˘

4.   Art thou not, fatal vision, sensible

     ˘ ‒ ˘   ‒ ˘   ‒   ˘ ‒   ˘ ‒

5.   To feeling as to sight, or art thou but

     ˘ ‒ ˘ ˘ ˘   ‒   ˘ ‒   ˘ ‒ ˘

6.   A dagger of the mind, a false creation

     ˘ ‒ ˘   ˘   ˘   ‒ ˘   ‒ ˘

7.   Proceeding from the heat-oppressed mind?"

Observe the first line: it has a regular alternation of light and accented syllables, yet there is an extra syllable at the end, making eleven syllables in the line, so it is not perfectly regular.

The second line has also the extra syllable; in addition the words *come, let* form a spondiac foot, ▬ ▬, so this line does not follow the iambic pattern exactly.

The third line is perfectly regular: just ten syllables, and all the feet are iambic.

The fourth line begins with an accented syllable, making the first foot trochaic, ▬ �”, while the second foot is spondaic, ▬ ▬ .

In the fifth line, the feet are all iambic, and there are no extra syllables.

In the sixth line, there is also a pyrrhic foot, made up of the words *of the;* there is also an extra syllable at the end.

In the seventh line, the second foot is a pyrrhic one.

Thus we find that of seven consecutive lines, only two follow the iambic pattern exactly. This is not a slip on the poet's part, it is intentional, to vary the music of the lines. A series of lines all alike in pattern would be very tiresome. The point to remember about meter, then, is that while the normal

pattern is iambic, it is allowable, and in fact necessary, to sub-
stitute either trochaic, spondaic or pyrrhic feet at any time,
and that by so substituting the poet gives a varied and pleas-
ing rhythm to his lines.

Dividing a line into metrical feet is called scanning. If you
would like to try this for yourself, take this passage:

"Stay, you imperfect speakers, tell me more.
By Sinel's death I know I am Thane of Glamis;
But how of Cawdor? The Thane of Cawdor lives,
A prosperous gentleman; and to be king
Stands not within the prospect of belief,
No more than to be Cawdor. Say from whence
You owe this strange intelligence, or why
Upon this blasted heath you stop our way
With such prophetic greeting? Speak, I charge you."

Copy this, leaving plenty of room between the lines. Now
read each line aloud, and as you read it, note which words or
syllables you accent, and mark them thus ━. Now mark all
the other syllables thus ⌣. Do this with each line in turn.
Then look at the first line, and divide your marks into groups
of two, thus:

━ ⌣   ⌣ ━   ⌣ ━   ⌣ ━   ⌣ ━

Note that the first foot is trochaic, the others iambic. Go on
with the other lines, and name each foot according to this
scheme:

━ ⌣ Trochaic.   ━ ━ Spondaic.
⌣ ━ Iambic.   ⌣ ⌣ Pyrrhic.

That is called scanning poetry. It is not a very important matter: one who writes poetry does not think of using iambic and trochaic feet, but he does have in mind a sort of pattern for his lines, and keeps more or less closely to it.

Not all parts of this play are in blank verse. The scenes where the witches appear are in a four-accent line, called tetrameter, and the lines rhyme. Turn to the first scene of the play and note the rhyme, and the short lines. Then there are a few passages in prose, such as the Porter's speech, Act II, Scene 3, and the dialogue between Lady Macduff and her son, Act IV, Scene 2. Shakespeare usually uses prose for humorous scenes, as he does here.

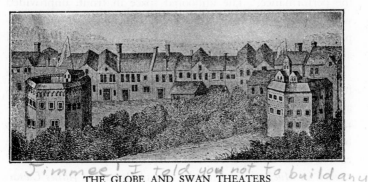

Jimmee! I told you not to build any more forts!

THE GLOBE AND SWAN THEATERS

THE ELIZABETHAN THEATER

In that mid-period when drama had left the shelter of the church and had not yet attained the haven of the theater, strolling bands of actors offered their wares in the courtyard of inns. It was natural, therefore, that when in 1574 James Burbage decided to build a permanent playhouse, he should follow the model he knew best. In the same way all the early theaters, The Curtain, The Globe, The Fortune, The Swan, The Rose, were built on the analogy of the inn courtyard.

Like this yard, the interior of the theater was open to the sky, except for the roofed galleries which extended around three sides. The stage projected out into the center, so that the audience practically surrounded the actors. To add to this difficulty, those who were willing to pay the price had seats upon the stage itself, and often hindered the course of the performance. The unfloored space in front, unprovided with seats, was occupied by the "groundlings," London apprentices and men of the poorer class who paid only a small admission fee. People of the middle class sat in the galleries.

The stage was equipped with no front curtain and no footlights. At the back, two doors led to the dressing rooms and served for exit and entrance. A small inner stage, separated from the larger one by a curtain, occupied a recess between these doors. It was used in various ways: for the casket scene in *The Merchant of Venice,* for the witches' cavern in *Macbeth,* and for the tent of Brutus in *Julius Cæsar*. It gave an opportunity to "set the stage" when action was still going on. Above this recess was a balcony, used for the musicians, for Juliet's balcony, for the hill in *Julius Cæsar,* for the wall of a town, the upper room in a house, or any other place where the action needed to be a little removed. Still higher than the balcony was the "hut" or small tower from which the flag was flown to announce the performance. A trap door, a canopy called the heavens, and various bits of stage machinery completed the resources of the Elizabethan stage.

Of scenery, there was very little. A desk, a bed, a throne or chair served to suggest the proper setting to the quick-witted audience. And if that were not enough, the author's careful description made all clear. Note how often Shakespeare's words announce the change of scene. Costumes were as elaborate as the resources of the company allowed but there

LADIES SELDOM ATTENDED THE PERFORMANCE AND ONLY
WHEN WELL MASKED

was no attempt at historical accuracy. Undoubtedly Julius Cæsar wore the doublet and hose of an Elizabethan gentleman and the Roman senators might easily pluck their hats about their brows.

Because of the lack of lighting facilities, plays were given in the afternoon. The flag flying from the hut would announce the performance and the audience would gather, coming on horseback across London Bridge or by boat over the river. The trumpet would sound and the prologue, dressed in black, would give a general idea of the play. In the absence of programs, this was necessary.

Then the play would begin. While the groundlings swayed and jostled in the pit, the gallants swaggered on the stage, and food venders plied their trade, the actors played their parts. They needed to be good to hold such an audience. Perhaps Richard Burbage, the best of them all, would please the groundlings with his Falstaff, or Shakespeare himself might take a part. No actresses would appear; boys took the women's parts; and no ladies attended the performance except occasionally and then well masked.

THE MODERN THEATER

WHAT changes the years have brought. The stage no longer thrusts out into the audience but has retired behind the proscenium arch. We sit, securely housed, in our comfortable seats in the orchestra, once the groundlings' pit, and we see the action as if we looked through a picture frame, into a three walled room. We are not now one with the actors; we are on-lookers, slightly aloof. Does this, perhaps, color our reactions?

Evidently it does and to the extent that, in the newer and larger theaters, an effort is being made to decrease, through architectural illusion, the actual distance between the audience and the stage.

Programs make the prologue unnecessary and long descriptions superfluous. The curtain rises to reveal new settings or falls to conceal awkward situations.

The two doors that were the sole means of exit and entrance have disappeared. Our actors come in from the wings, or the garden, or the next room. It is not necessary to mark their movements by rhyme tags, or sennets.

Costumes are meticulously accurate. Stage machinery has infinitely multiplied; all the magic resources of color and light are at hand. Only in one respect are we reverting to something like Elizabethan practice. Our scenery is becoming increasingly simple.

There was a time when realism was demanded. We must have authentic palaces for Macbeth, real graveyards for Ophelia, actual Roman Forums for Cæsar. But the reaction has set in. Suggestion rather than realism is the ideal. It was discovered that sometimes the scenery got in the way of the action, and that greater flexibility as well as more imaginative reaction could be gained by simpler means. Setting aside the rather bald performances of such troops as the *Ben Greet Players,* we may yet find many a more pretentious and artistic production using a single stage setting. The very beautiful presentation of *Hamlet* by Norman Bel Geddes was a case in point. With the lavish use of lights and a few trifling changes in properties, the same background represented the Danish battlements, the king's palace, Ophelia's grave, and Gertrude's boudoir.

The modern stage has both gained and lost. It has gained infinitely in historical accuracy, in variety of effects, in picturesqueness. But it has lost something of the close association between actor and audience, and something of robust, whole-hearted appraisal. It would be interesting if we could, for a moment, be transported back to a Shakespearean playhouse. Perhaps then we might decide where the advantage lies.

BIOGRAPHICAL NOTES

EUGENE GLADSTONE O'NEILL

BORN on Broadway not far from the scene of his later triumphs, the son of one of the most impressive personalities of
the stage of his time, it is no wonder Eugene O'Neill is to-
day one of the theater's most commanding figures. From his
entrance into life on October 16, 1888 at the Barrett House,
now the Hotel Cadillac on Broadway and 43d Street, until
the age of seven, O'Neill was closely associated with the
theater for he accompanied his parents, Ella Quinlan and
James O'Neill on road shows of his famous *Monte Cristo*.
It is not surprising then that young O'Neill became acquainted
with every phase of the theater long before he knew his mul-
tiplication tables.

After his seventh birthday, Eugene attended Catholic and
non-sectarian boarding schools and in 1902 entered Betts
Academy where he remained until graduation in 1906. The
following autumn he entered Princeton but was expelled
shortly before final examinations in June because of "general
hell-raising." Although the offense was not too serious to
prevent his return the following Fall, college no longer interested him, and he left to take a position in a New York
Mail Order house. This firm, specializing in "Ten Cent
Jewelry . . . giving an alleged phonograph with one record

as a premium to children and seminary girls who disposed of the shabby baubles" soon went out of business much to the relief of O'Neill, who had never taken the work seriously.

In 1909, he married Kathleen Jenkins of New York and a son, Eugene, was born the following year. This marriage which O'Neill characterized as a "mistake" was one of short duration and was formally ended by divorce in 1912.

The following years, spent in travel and experimentation with various phases of life, were to provide a rich background on which he could later draw. First came a prospecting trip to Spanish Honduras for gold; on his return in 1910, a brief engagement as assistant manager in his father's theatrical company and then another voyage to Buenos Aires. This was followed by the holding of small jobs in South America, further ventures on the high seas, tending mules on a cattle boat, small parts in his father's theatrical productions and reporting for newspapers. During this period his favorite authors were Jack London, Conrad and Kipling but on his trips he was "no literary chap in search of copy." He preferred hanging about the water front, making friends with sailors, stevedores and outcasts. He worked where he could find work to provide money for board, room and drink and the crude forms of entertainment one could find around the wharves.

As a result of this irregular living, his health broke down and in December, 1912, he entered Gaylord Sanitarium at Wallingford, Connecticut, with a touch of tuberculosis. The five months spent at Gaylord marked the turning point in his life. He had time to read and think. He decided he wanted to write plays. The youth who entered Gaylord Sanitarium and the man who left were two different beings. In the next sixteen months he regained his health, read widely, particularly the Greek, Elizabethan and modern plays, especially Strindberg. He also wrote eleven one-act plays, two long ones and some verse. Someone suggested that he might improve his technical knowledge and in the Fall of 1914, at the insistence of his friend, Clayton Hamilton, O'Neill entered Professor Baker's famous *English 47* class in Playwriting at Harvard. Of his association with Baker, O'Neill has commented in his own words: "Yes, I did get a great deal from Baker, personally. He encouraged me, made me feel it was worth while going ahead. My association with him meant a devil of a lot to me at that time."

O'Neill spent the following winter of 1915-1916 in the Bohemian atmosphere of Greenwich village associating with Radicals, I.W.W.'s, native villagers, Negroes and Italians of the quarter. It was not until returning to Provincetown that summer that he became affiliated with the group who were destined to produce his earlier plays. That summer, in the light of the Old Wharf Theater they put on *Bound East for Cardiff* with O'Neill in the rôle of the Second Mate.

After the summer season they returned to New York, organized as the Provincetown Players and opened the Playwrights Theater on Macdougal street. The venture met with success, and there during the next four years all but one of O'Neill's one-act plays were produced. It was here, too, that

The Emperor Jones was first presented November 3, 1920. Meanwhile O'Neill was gaining recognition from publishers and Broadway producers. Mencken and George Jean Nathan who were then editing the *Smart Set,* published *The Long Voyage Home, Ile* and the *Moon of the Caribbees* in their magazine.

In 1918 he married Agnes Boulton. There are two children, a son and daughter. In 1928 he visited Shanghai and the Far East where he was reported ill. However he returned to France, and established a residence at Château du Plesis, Saint Antoine-du-Rocher near Tours. There he was granted a divorce and shortly after married Carlotta Monterey, an actress. They returned to New York in the fall of 1931 and moved into a new home on an island off the coast of Georgia. Eugene O'Neill died in Boston on November 27, 1953.

o'neill's works

Since the production of his first full length play, *Beyond the Horizon* in 1920, O'Neill's position as the outstanding American dramatist has not been seriously challenged. He has four times received the Pulitzer Prize, and once the medal for artistic achievement by the American Academy of Arts and Sciences. He also received the Nobel Prize for Literature in 1936. O'Neill is very well known abroad, his plays having been produced in every major country of the world.

His plays are:

The Web—*1914*

Thirst—*1914*

Recklessness—*1914*

Warnings—*1914*

Bound East for Cardiff—*1916*

Abortion—*1916*

Before Breakfast—*1916*

The Long Voyage Home
   —*1917*

The Sniper—*1917*

In the Zone—*1917*

Ile—*1917*

Where the Cross is Made
   —*1918*

The Rope—*1918*

The Moon of the Caribbees
   —*1918*

The Dreamy Kid—*1919*

Beyond the Horizon—*1920*

Chris—*1920*

Exorcism—*1920*

Gold—*1920*

The Emperor Jones—*1920*

Diff'rent—*1920*

Anna Christie—*1921*

The Straw—*1921*

The First Man—*1922*

The Hairy Ape—*1922*

Welded—*1924*

All God's Chillun Got
   Wings—*1924*

The Rime of the Ancient
   Mariner—*1925*

Desire Under the Elms—*1925*

The Fountain—*1925*

The Great God Brown—*1926*

Marco Millions—*1927*

Lazarus Laughed—*1927*

Strange Interlude—*1928*

Dynamo—*1929*

Mourning Becomes Electra
   —*1931*

Ah, Wilderness—*1933*

Days Without End—*1934*

The Iceman Cometh—*1946*

A Moon for the Misbegotten—*1952*

Long Day's Journey Into the Night—*1956*

A Touch of the Poet—*1958*

SOURCES OF THE EMPEROR JONES

O'NEILL has told the story of the play's origin in an interview.

"The idea of *The Emperor Jones* came from an old circus man I knew. This man told me a story, current in Hayti, concerning the late President Sam. This was to the effect that Sam had said they'd never get him with a lead bullet, that he would get himself first with a silver one. . . . This notion about the silver bullet struck me and I made note of the story. About six months later I got the idea of the woods, but I couldn't see how it could be done on the stage, and I passed it up again. A year elapsed. One day I was reading of religious feasts in the Congo and the uses to which the drum is put there: how it starts at a normal pulse and is slowly intensified until the heartbeat of everyone present corresponds to the frenzied beat of the drum. There was an idea and an experiment. How would this sort of thing work on an audience in a theater? The effect of the tropical forest on the human imagination was honestly come by. It was the result of my own experience while prospecting for gold in Spanish Honduras."—*New York World, November 9, 1924.*

What effect the tom-toms had on the audience is well expressed by Mr. Walkley writing in the *London Times:*

34

THE CHAIN GANG SCENE
FROM THE PRODUCTION AT THE TACOMA LITTLE THEATRE

"Great is the influence of rhythm. A persistent drum beat punctuates *The Emperor Jones,* beginning slowly, quickening as scene follows scene, culminating in a headlong prestissimo, but never ceasing for a moment, not even in the intervals between scenes. Of course your nerves are affected. You throb responsive to the drum. You have a feeling of tense expectation. Finally you are exasperated and yearn only for relief from the persistent agonizing sound. It is a nightmare.

"The whole thing is one eerie sensation, a brutal attack on the nerves, yet with an inherent nobility, an impression of power in its eponymous hero that redeems it. It is a superb performance, a triumph of the uncanny that you fear will haunt you long."

PRESENTATION

The Play

The Emperor Jones was first produced by the Provincetown Players at the Playwrights Theater, Macdougal Street, New York, and immediately stamped O'Neill as a coming dramatist and earned for him widespread recognition. The play, well staged, well directed and with the prominent negro actor, Charles Gilpin, as the Emperor was a tremendous success.

The *New York Post* of November 3, 1920, has an interesting article on its production—

"The Provincetown Players are fortunate in having a contribution from Eugene O'Neill to start them off, for, however highly special this man can be without half trying, his work always has that in it which commands interest.

"It is so with *The Emperor Jones,* a study of fear in the tropics in eight scenes, five pistol shots and several hundred thousand taps on a tom-tom. . . . For the most part the play is carried on by the soliloquies of one man, the ex-Pullman car porter, who has hoodwinked the natives into thinking him an Emperor. But they tire of his rule and show their dissatisfaction by preparations to murder him. He is shown at different stages of his flight through the jungle with his early confidence giving place to fear, then terror, then semi-madness and with hallucinations of his past life appearing

36

before him. He wanders back to his starting place and the enraged natives kill him with silver bullets they have molded to pierce his supposedly invulnerable body.

"Eugene O'Neill always has in his bag of tricks the means of communicating to his audience the feelings of his characters. At some well devised moment the devastating terror of Jones is made gripping and real. That the illusion is greatly aided by imaginative setting and lighting is an agreeable discovery. That so competent a player as Charles Gilpin, the negro actor, lately seen in John Drinkwater's *Abraham Lincoln* should lend the piece authority was more or less to be expected."

And when the play was transferred to the Selwyn it was no less highly praised. The *New York Times* reports, December 28th, 1920:

"Transferred to the larger and better equipped stage of the Selwyn, O'Neill's exciting and terrifying play about a night flight of a Negro through a fever-steeped and panicky jungle in the tropics is unfolded with illusive beauty."

The Emperor Jones has also been produced with Paul Robeson in the principal rôle both here and abroad and audiences all over the world have been terrified and thrilled by the play's weird spell.

The Opera

"*The Emperor Jones* triumphs as an opera—World premiere of Louis Gruenberg's version of O'Neill's play hailed at the Metropolitan—Tibbett superb in the rôle"—This is the way the *New York Times* hailed the production of the opera at the Metropolitan on January 7, 1933.

For the greater part of the seven scenes the opera follows the play but in the final scene Gruenberg substituted one of his own which makes the play no less effective.

Describing this scene the *New York Herald Tribune* says: "The practical agents of Jones' doom, who shoot him down in O'Neill's last act, become in the opera, an agency more symbolic and even in presence more Greek. The chorus placed in the orchestra pit, or immovable and decorative on the stage, is practically invisible to the audience. In the orchestral prelude the voices rise from the pit condemning Jones 'Dis Man Muss Die' and swearing vengeance upon him. As the opera proceeds at certain special moments the chorus reiterates threats and prophecies, with the effect of an immense crescendo. As this motive of retribution develops and gains in power, the bodies of the blacks emerge from the orchestra, looming higher and higher over the rim of the stage, until at last the witch-doctor jumps over the footlights, pointing to Jones, dancing his fiendish dance, and all the negroes, swinging and swaying, close in upon his black majesty. Whipping out his pistol with the last bullet of silver Jones kills himself. The negroes cautiously approach the inert body, prod it with their bayonets, lift it on their shoulders, and disappear in the forest. The savage triumphal songs of four tribes intermingle, grow fainter, echo from the distance. The stage is silent and empty as the curtain falls."

COMPARATIVE STUDY

CLOSELY linked by common elements of ambition, fear, superstition, degradation, destiny and tragedy yet widely separated by age, authorship, diction and dramatic form, the comparison of William Shakespeare's *Macbeth* and Eugene O'Neill's *The Emperor Jones* offers a fascinating study.

Both plays have strong central characters in Macbeth and Jones. Both men are impelled by an overwhelming sense of ambition and fear. Both rest secure in prophecies; Macbeth in the Witch's assurance that no man born of woman can harm him and that he is safe until Birnam Wood shall come to Dunsinane Hill; Jones in the fact that the natives fully believe he is invulnerable except to silver bullets. Both are terrified by apparitions and are pursued by their own fears and superstitions.

With these points of contact, the careful student will be able to discover other similarities and contrasts, to show how the prophecies are fulfilled in each case, to compare the chief characters, to trace the falling action of each play, and to show in what way the plays are, or are not, alike. It is hoped that he will, perhaps, distinguish between the surface differences that are inseparable from the age to which they belong and the essential unity of vital truths, wherever and whenever manifested. When he sees the classic and the modern author molding their products in different workshops and possibly with varying degrees of skill but out of the same material, the age-old clay of human nature, he may learn how indestructible are the qualities of sincerity, clear vision, and artistry that go to make up a masterpiece.

As an aid to the student in drawing a comparison the editor has included questions for a comparative study. Stage directions and description of sets from the best modern productions prefix the scenes in *Macbeth* and *The Emperor Jones* to assure a more accurate visualization. To these have been added, for the guidance of such pupils and the convenience of such teachers as desire them, certain study helps, suggestions and tests for an intensive study of each play. The experienced teacher will know how to make these of use and yet subordinate to the fundamental aim, comparison and enjoyment of the two plays.

THE TRAGEDY OF MACBETH

By

William Shakespeare

THE CHARACTERS IN THE PLAY

DUNCAN, *King of Scotland.*

MALCOLM,
DONALBAIN, } *his sons.*

MACBETH,
BANQUO, } *Generals of the King's army.*

MACDUFF,
LENNOX,
ROSS,
MENTEITH, } *Noblemen of Scotland.*
ANGUS,
CAITHNESS,

FLEANCE, *son to Banquo.*

SIWARD, *Earl of Northumberland, General of the English forces.*

Young SIWARD, *his son.*

Boy, *son to Macduff.*

SEYTON, *an officer attending on Macbeth.*

An English Doctor.

A Scotch Doctor.

A Sergeant.

A Porter.

An Old Man.

LADY MACBETH.

LADY MACDUFF.

A Gentlewoman, attending on Lady Macbeth.

HECATE.

Three Witches.

Apparitions.

Lords, Gentlemen, Officers, Soldiers, Murderers, Attendants, and Messengers.

SCENE: *Scotland; England.*

MACBETH
FROM THE SCREEN PRODUCTION

The Tragedy of Macbeth

ACT FIRST

SCENE I

A desolate open place, with no grass, but low stunted bushes
here and there. Dark clouds cover the sky, thunder rolls,
and lightning flashes. Three strange beings appear: they
have the form of women, with withered faces, gleaming
eyes, and torn and disordered clothing. They join hands
and circle about, then stop and speak.

First Witch. When shall we three meet again?
　　In thunder, lightning, or in rain?
Second Witch. When the hurlyburly's done,
　　When the battle's lost and won.
Third Witch. That will be ere the set of sun.　　　　5
First Witch. Where the place?
Second Witch.　　　　　　　　　　　Upon the **heath.**
Third Witch. There to meet with Macbeth.
First Witch. I come, Graymalkin!
Second Witch. Paddock calls.
Third Witch. Anon.

3. **Hurlyburly**—Uproar.
8. **Graymalkin**—A gray cat.
8. **Paddock**—A toad. The cat and the toad were evil spirits in the form
　　of animals, who now summon the witches.
8. **Anon**—I'm coming.

All. Fair is foul, and foul is fair;
  Hover through the fog and filthy air.   [*Exeunt.* 10

Scene II

*The King's camp near Forres. Tents scattered about; in the
  foreground a large tent belonging to the King, with a
  soldier on guard. Other soldiers near by: they wear the
  Scottish plaid, a loose outer garment reaching to the knee,
  held in by a belt; stockings coming above the calf of the
  leg, leaving the knee bare. They are armed with spears,
  swords, or battle-axes, and carry shields covered with
  tough hide. The officers and the* King's *sons wear
  armor;* Duncan, *an elderly man, wears a long mantle.
  Shouts and the hurried beating of a drum are heard, at
  which* Duncan, *his sons* Malcolm *and* Donalbain *come
  out of the King's tent; they see a bleeding sergeant approaching.*

Duncan. What bloody man is that? He can report,
  As seemeth by his plight, of the revolt
  The newest state.
Malcolm. This is the sergeant
  Who like a good and hardy soldier fought
  'Gainst my captivity.—Hail, brave friend!   5
  Say to the king thy knowledge of the broil

As thou didst leave it.

Sergeant.   Doubtful it stood;
As two spent swimmers, that do cling together
And choke their art. The merciless Macdonwald—
Worthy to be a rebel, for to that   10
The multiplying villanies of nature
Do swarm upon him!—from the western isles
Of kerns and gallowglasses is supplied:
And Fortune, on his damnèd quarrel smiling,
Showed like a rebel's whore: but all 's too weak;   15
For brave Macbeth—well he deserves that name!—
Disdaining fortune, with his brandished steel,
Which smoked with bloody execution,
Like valor's minion carved out his passage,
Till he faced the slave;   20
Which ne'er shook hands, nor bade farewell to him,
Till he unseamed him from the nave to the chops,
And fixed his head upon our battlements.

Duncan. O valiant cousin! worthy gentleman!

Sergeant. As whence the sun 'gins his reflection   25
Shipwrecking storms and direful thunders break,
So from that spring whence comfort seemed to come
Discomfort swells. Mark, King of Scotland, mark:—
No sooner justice had, with valor armed,

13. **Kerns**—Light-armed foot soldiers, carrying daggers and darts.
13. **Gallowglasses**—Heavy-armed foot soldiers.
14. **Fortune**—Fortune at first smiled upon him, then deserted him.
21. **Which**—Who.
24. **Cousin**—Duncan and Macbeth were first cousins.

Compelled these skipping kerns to trust their heels, 30
But the Norweyan lord, surveying vantage,
With furbished arms and new supplies of men,
Began a fresh assault.
Duncan. Dismayed not this
Our captains, Macbeth and Banquo?
Sergeant. Yes;
As sparrows eagles, or the hare the lion. 35
If I say sooth, I must report they were
As cannons overcharged with double cracks; so they
Doubly redoubled strokes upon the foe.
Except they meant to bathe in reeking wounds,
Or memorize another Golgotha, 40
I cannot tell.
But I am faint; my gashes cry for help.
Duncan. So well thy words become thee as thy wounds;
They smack of honor both. Go get him surgeons.

[*Exit* Sergeant, *attended.*

Enter Ross.

Who comes here?
Malcolm. The worthy Thane of Ross. 45
Lennox. What haste looks through his eyes! So should
he look
That seems to speak things strange.

31. **Norweyan lord**—Sweno, King of Norway had invaded Scotland.
31. **Surveying vantage**—Seeing his opportunity.
32. **Furbished**—Newly polished.
40. **Golgotha**—The hill where Christ was crucified; hence, to make this
spot as memorable as Golgotha.

Ross.   God save the king!

Duncan. Whence camest thou, worthy Thane?

Ross.   From Fife, great King;
  Where the Norweyan banners flout the sky
  And fan our people cold. Norway himself,   50
  With terrible numbers,—
  Assisted by that most disloyal traitor,
  The Thane of Cawdor began a dismal conflict;
  Till that Bellona's bridegroom, lapped in proof,
  Confronted him with self-comparisons,   55
  Point against point, rebellious arm 'gainst arm,
  Curbing his lavish spirit; and, to conclude,
  The victory fell on us.

Duncan.   Great happiness!

Ross.   —That now
  Sweno, the Norways' King, craves composition;
  Nor would we deign him burial of his men   60
  Till he disbursèd, at Saint Colme's Inch,
  Ten thousand dollars to our general use.

Duncan. No more that thane of Cawdor shall deceive
  Our bosom interest. Go pronounce his present death,
  And with his former title greet Macbeth.   65

Ross. I'll see it done.

Duncan. What he hath lost noble Macbeth hath won.

                                        [*Exeunt.*

54. **Bellona's bridegroom**—Bellona was the goddess of war; her bride-
    groom would be Mars, god of war: Ross calls Macbeth Mars.
54. **Lapped in proof**—Clad in strong armor.
55. **Confronted him, etc.**—Met him with equal strength.
60. **Composition**—Terms of peace.

Purpose:

Scene III

The place is the same as in the first scene. The storm is over,
but distant thunder is heard. The three Witches *enter*
from different directions; when they hear the drum, they
join hands and circle about as they chant their chorus.
Macbeth *and* Banquo *are men of middle age, but vigor-*
ous. They wear linked coats of mail, and walk slowly,
wearied after the battle.

First Witch. Where hast thou been, Sister?
Second Witch. Killing swine.
Third Witch. Sister, where thou?
First Witch. A sailor's wife had chestnuts in her lap,
    And munched, and munched, and munched. "Give
      me," quoth I.　　　　　　　　　　　　　　　　5
    "Aroint thee, witch!" the rump-fed ronyon cries.
    Her husband's to Aleppo gone, master o' the *Tiger;*
    But in a sieve I'll thither sail,
    And, like a rat without a tail,
    I'll do, I'll do, and I'll do.　　　　　　　　　　10
Second Witch. I'll give thee a wind.

---

2. **Killing swine**—It was commonly believed that witches had the power
    to cause the death of animals.
6. **Aroint-thee**—Away with thee!
6. **Rump-fed ronyon**—A scurvy, scabby person, fed on scraps.
11. **I'll give thee a wind**—Witches could control winds, and tempests.

First Witch. Thou 'rt kind.

Third Witch. And I another.

First Witch. I myself have all the other;
    And the very ports they blow,   15
    All the quarters that they know
    I' the shipman's card.
    I will drain him dry as hay:
    Sleep shall neither night nor day
    Hang upon his pent-house lid;   20
    He shall live a man forbid:
    Weary se'nnights nine times nine
    Shall he dwindle, peak, and pine
    Though his bark cannot be lost,
    Yet it shall be tempest-tost.   25
    Look what I have.

Second Witch. Show me, show me.

First Witch. Here I have a pilot's thumb,
    Wrack'd as homeward he did come.   *[Drum within.*

Third Witch. A drum, a drum!   30
    Macbeth doth come.

All. The weird Sisters, hand in hand,
    Posters of the sea and land,
    Thus do go about, about;
    Thrice to thine and thrice to mine,   35

15. **Ports they blow**—The ports into which the winds carry vessels.
17. **Shipman's card**—The card in a compass.
20. **Pent-house lid**—A shed with a sloping roof; here means eyelid.
21. **Forbid**—Under a curse.
33. **Posters**—Those who ride post, i.e., travel with great speed.

And thrice again, to make up nine.
Peace! the charm's wound up.

Enter MACBETH *and* BANQUO.

Macbeth. So foul and fair a day I have not seen.
Banquo. How far is't called to Forres? What are these
So withered, and so wild in their attire,   40
That look not like the inhabitants o' the earth,
And yet are on't? Live you? or are you aught
That man may question? You seem to understand
me,
By each at once her choppy finger laying
Upon her skinny lips: you should be women,   45
And yet your beards forbid me to interpret
That you are so.
Macbeth.   Speak, if you can—What are you?
First Witch. All hail, Macbeth! hail to thee, Thane of
Glamis!
Second Witch. All hail, Macbeth! hail to thee, Thane of
Cawdor!
Third Witch. All hail, Macbeth, that shalt be King here-
after!   50
Banquo. Good sir, why do you start; and seem to fear
Things that do sound so fair? I' the name of truth,
Are ye fantastical, or that indeed
Which outwardly ye show? My noble partner

53. **Fantastical**—Imaginary.

You greet with present grace and great prediction   55
Of noble having and of royal hope,
That he seems rapt withal; to me you speak not.
If you can look into the seeds of time,
And say which grain will grow and which will not,
Speak then to me, who neither beg nor fear   60
Your favors nor your hate.

First Witch. Hail!

Second Witch. Hail!

Third Witch. Hail!

First Witch. Lesser than Macbeth, and greater.   65

Second Witch. Not so happy, yet much happier.

Third Witch. Thou shalt get kings, though thou be none.
    So all hail, Macbeth and Banquo!

First Witch. Banquo and Macbeth, all hail!

Macbeth. Stay, you imperfect speakers, tell me more.   70
    By Sinel's death I know I am Thane of Glamis;
    But how of Cawdor? the Thane of Cawdor lives,
    A prosperous gentleman; and to be king
    Stands not within the prospect of belief,
    No more than to be Cawdor. Say from whence   75
    You owe this strange intelligence? Or why
    Upon this blasted heath you stop our way
    With such prophetic greeting? Speak, I charge you.
                                    [Witches *vanish.*

55. **Grace**—Favor.
56. **Noble having**—Prediction of large possessions, and of becoming king.
57. **Rapt withal**—Completely absorbed by it.
67. **Get kings**—Be the father of kings.
71. **Sinel**—Macbeth's father.

Banquo. The earth hath bubbles, as the water has,
    And these are of them. Whither are they vanished?   80
Macbeth. Into the air, and what seemed corporal melted
    As breath into the wind. Would they had stayed!
Banquo. Were such things here as we do speak about?
    Or have we eaten on the insane root
    That takes the reason prisoner?   85
Macbeth. Your children shall be kings.
Banquo.   You shall be King.
Macbeth. And Thane of Cawdor, too; went it not so?
Banquo. To the selfsame tune and words. Who's here?

noblemen   *Enter* Ross *and* Angus.

Ross. The King hath happily received, Macbeth,
    The news of thy success; and when he reads   90
    Thy personal venture in the rebels' fight,
    His wonders and his praises do contend
    Which should be thine or his. Silenced with that,
    In viewing o'er the rest o' the selfsame day,
    He finds thee in the stout Norweyan ranks,   95
    Nothing afeard of what thyself didst make,
    Strange images of death. As thick as hail
    Came post with post; and every one did bear
    Thy praises in his Kingdom's great defence,

81. **Corporal**—Having real bodies.
84. **Insane root**—The root that causes insanity.
91. **The rebels' fight**—The fight against the rebels.
92. **His wonders**—His wonder at your deeds makes him forget to praise.
98. **Came post with post**—Messengers came as fast as one could count.

And pour'd them down before him.

Angus.   We are sent   100
    To give thee from our royal master thanks;
    Only to herald thee into his sight,
    Not pay thee.

Ross. And, for an earnest of a greater honor,
    He bade me, from him, call thee Thane of Cawdor: 105
    In which addition, hail, most worthy Thane!
    For it is thine.

Banquo. [*Aside*]   What, can the devil speak true?

Macbeth. The Thane of Cawdor lives: why do you dress
    me
    In borrowed robes?

Angus.   Who was the Thane, lives yet;
    But under heavy judgment bears that life   110
    Which he deserves to lose. Whether he was combined
    With those of Norway, or did line the rebel
    With hidden help and vantage, or that with both
    He labored in his country's wrack, I know not;
    But treasons capital, confessed and proved,   115
    Have overthrown him.

Macbeth. [*Aside*]   Glamis, and Thane of Cawdor!
    The greatest is behind.
    —Thanks for your pains.
    —Do you not hope your children shall be kings,
    When those that gave the Thane of Cawdor to me

104. **Earnest**—An advance payment.
106. **Addition**—Title of honor.
112. **Line**—Strengthen.

Promised no less to them?

Banquo.   That, trusted home,   120
 Might yet enkindle you unto the crown,
 Besides the Thane of Cawdor. But 't is strange:
 And oftentimes, to win us to our harm,
 The instruments of darkness tell us truths;
 Win us with honest trifles, to betray 's   125
 In deepest consequence.
 Cousins, a word, I pray you.

Macbeth. [*Aside*]   Two truths are told,
 As happy prologues to the swelling act
 Of the imperial theme.—I thank you, gentlemen.
 [*Aside*] This supernatural soliciting   130
 Cannot be ill, cannot be good; if ill,
 Why hath it given me earnest of success,
 Commencing in a truth? I am Thane of Cawdor:
 If good, why do I yield to that suggestion
 Whose horrid image doth unfix my hair   135
 And make my seated heart knock at my ribs,
 Against the use of nature? Present fears
 Are less than horrible imaginings;
 My thought, whose murder yet is but fantastical,
 Shakes so my single state of man that function   140
 Is smothered in surmise, and nothing is

120. **Trusted home**—Trusted completely.
126. **Deepest consequence**—Matters of the greatest importance.
128. **Happy prologues**—Happy introductions to the coronation.
135. **Unfix my hair**—Cause it to stand on end.
140. **Single**—Weak.

But what is not.

Banquo.   Look, how our partner's rapt!

Macbeth. [*Aside*] If chance will have me King, why, chance may crown me,

Without my stir.

Banquo.   New honors come upon him,

Like our strange garments, cleave not to their mold 145

But with the aid of use.

Macbeth. [*Aside*]   Come what come may,

Time and the hour runs through the roughest day.

Banquo. Worthy Macbeth, we stay upon your leisure.

Macbeth. Give me your favor: my dull brain was wrought

With things forgotten. Kind gentlemen, your pains 150

Are registered where every day I turn

The leaf to read them. Let us toward the King.

Think upon what hath chanced, and at more time,

The interim having weighed it, let us speak

Our free hearts each to other.

Banquo.   Very gladly.   155

Macbeth. Till then, enough. Come friends.   [*Exeunt.*

142. **Rapt**—Absorbed.
145. **Strange garments**—New clothes.
148. **Stay upon**—Await your pleasure.
154. **The interim, etc.**—Having considered it meanwhile. The last three
    lines of Macbeth's speech are spoken to Banquo.

Scene IV

Forres. A room in Duncan's *castle. A large room, with stone
walls and floor; rushes are strewn on the floor. A flourish
of trumpets is heard, the customary way of announcing
the arrival of an important personage.* Duncan *enters,
wearing a crown and a richly embroidered robe; he is
followed by* Malcolm, Donalbain, Lennox *and attendants.* Duncan *seats himself in a great chair, the others
group themselves at either side of him.*

Duncan. Is execution done on Cawdor? Are not
Those in commission yet returned?

Malcolm.   My liege,
They are not yet come back. But I have spoke
With one that saw him die; who did report
That very frankly he confessed his treasons,   5
Implored your Highness' pardon and set forth
A deep repentance. Nothing in his life
Became him like the leaving it; he died
As one that had been studied in his death
To throw away the dearest thing he owed,   10
As 'twere a careless trifle.

Duncan.   There's no art
To find the mind's construction in the face;

9. **Studied**—Had made it a study.
10. **Owed**—Owned.
12. **To find, etc.**—There is no art to tell what is in a person's mind by
his face.

He was a gentleman on whom I built   *IRONY*
An absolute trust.
   Enter Macbeth, Banquo, Ross, *and* Angus.
      O worthiest cousin!
The sin of my ingratitude even now   15
Was heavy on me; thou art so far before
That swiftest wing of recompense is slow
To overtake thee. Would thou hadst less deserved,
That the proportion both of thanks and payment
Might have been mine! Only I have left to say,   20
More is thy due than more than all can pay.
Macbeth. The service and the loyalty I owe,
 In doing it, pays itself. Your Highness' part
 Is to receive our duties; and our duties
 Are to your throne and state children and servants; 25
 Which do but what they should, by doing every thing
 Safe toward your love and honor.
Duncan.   Welcome hither:
 I have begun to plant thee, and will labor
 To make thee full of growing. Noble Banquo,
 That hast no less deserved, nor must be known   30
 No less to have done so; let me infold thee
 And hold thee to my heart.
Banquo.   There if I grow,

19. **That the proportion, etc.**—That both my thanks and my payment
  might be in due proportion to what you deserve.
22. **The service and the loyalty**—The loyal service.
27. **Safe towards, etc.**—Everything that tends to make safe your loved
  and honored self.

The harvest is your own.

Duncan.   My plenteous joys,
Wanton in fulness, seek to hide themselves
In drops of sorrow. Sons, kinsmen, thanes,   35
And you whose places are the nearest, know
We will establish our estate upon
Our eldest, Malcolm, whom we name hereafter
The Prince of Cumberland; which honor must
Not unaccompanied invest him only,   40
But signs of nobleness, like stars, shall shine
On all deservers. From hence to Inverness,
And bind us further to you.

Macbeth. The rest is labor, which is not used for you:
I 'll be myself the harbinger and make joyful   45
The hearing of my wife with your approach;
So humbly take my leave.

Duncan.   My worthy Cawdor!

Macbeth. [*Aside*] The Prince of Cumberland! that is a
          step
On which I must fall down, or else o'erleap,
For in my way it lies. Stars, hide your fires;   50
Let not light see my black and deep desires:
The eye wink at the hand; yet let that be
Which the eye fears, when it is done, to see.   [*Exit.*

37. **Establish our estate**—Settle the succession to the throne.
42. **Inverness**—Where Macbeth's castle stood.
44. **The rest, etc.**—All that I do that is not done for you is tiresome.
50. **For in my way**—Malcolm was an obstacle to Macbeth.
50. **Stars**—Macbeth is thinking of something that will be done at night.

Duncan. True, worthy Banquo; he is full so valiant,
　　And in his commendations I am fed;　　　　　　　55
　　It is a banquet to me. Let 's after him,
　　Whose care is gone before to bid us welcome:
　　It is a peerless kinsman.　　　　　[*Flourish. Exeunt.*

Scene V

Inverness. A room in Macbeth's *castle. The walls are of
stone, the windows high and narrow; heavy benches and
chairs at side. The general impression is cold and com-
fortless.* Lady Macbeth *enters. She wears a long flowing
gown with a girdle; over it a rich mantle, clasped with a
brooch. She holds a letter in her hand, and reads
excitedly.*

Lady Macbeth. "They met me in the day of success;
and I have learned by the perfectest report, they have more in
them than mortal knowledge. When I burned in desire to
question them further, they made themselves air, into which
they vanished. Whiles I stood rapt in the wonder of it, came
missives from the King, who all-hailed me 'Thane of Cawdor'; by which title, before, these weird sisters saluted me, and
referred me to the coming-on of time, with 'Hail, king that
shalt be!' This have I thought good to deliver thee, my

54. **He is**—Macbeth is. Banquo has been praising Macbeth to Duncan.
　2. **Perfectest report**—Most accurate information.
　6. **Missives**—Messengers.

dearest partner of greatness, that thou mightst not lose the
dues of rejoicing, by being ignorant of what greatness is promised thee. Lay it to thy heart, and farewell."

Glamis thou art, and Cawdor; and shalt be   15
What thou art promised. Yet do I fear thy nature;
It is too full o' the milk of human kindness
To catch the nearest way. Thou wouldst be great;
Art not without ambition, but without
The illness should attend it. ⌈What thou wouldst
  highly,   20
That wouldst thou holily; wouldst not play false,
And yet wouldst wrongly win. ⌉Thou'ldst have, great
  Glamis,
That which cries, "Thus thou must do! if thou have it";
And that which rather thou dost fear to do
Than wishest should be undone. Hie thee hither, 25
That I may pour my spirits in thine ear,
And chastise with the valor of my tongue
All that impedes thee from the golden round,
Which fate and metaphysical aid doth seem
To have thee crowned withal.

Enter a MESSENGER.

What is your tidings? 30

Messenger. The King comes here tonight.

17. **Human kindness**—Human nature.
20. **Illness**—Evil.
23. **That which cries**—i.e. The crown cries.
28. **Golden round**—The crown.
29. **Metaphysical**—Supernatural.

Lady Macbeth.   Thou'rt mad to say it!
　　Is not thy master with him? Who, were't so,
　　Would have informed for preparatïon.
Messenger. So please you, it is true. Our Thane is coming;
　　One of my fellows had the speed of him,   35
　　Who, almost dead for breath, had scarcely more
　　Than would make up his message.
Lady Macbeth.   Give him tending;
　　He brings great news.   [*Exit* Messenger.
　　⌈The raven himself is hoarse⌉
　　That croaks the fatal entrance of Duncan
　　Under my battlements.—Come, you spirits   40
　　That tend on mortal thoughts, unsex me here;
　　And fill me, from the crown to the toe, top-full
　　Of direst cruelty! make thick my blood;
　　Stop up the access and passage to remorse,
　　That no compunctious visitings of nature   45
　　Shake my fell purpose, nor keep peace between
　　The effect and it! Come to my woman's breasts,
　　And take my milk for gall, you murdering ministers,
　　Wherever in your sightless substances
　　You wait on nature's mischief! Come, thick night,   5c
　　And pall thee in the dunnest smoke of hell,
　　That my keen knife see not the wound it makes,

35. **Had the speed of**—Outstripped him.
41. **Mortal**—Deadly.
48. **Take my milk**—Turn my milk into gall.
48. **Murdering ministers**—Agents of murder.
49. **Sightless substances**—Invisible forms.

Nor heaven peep through the blanket of the dark,
To cry, "Hold, hold!"

Enter MACBETH.

                Great Glamis! worthy Cawdor!
Greater than both, by the all-hail hereafter!   55
Thy letters have transported me beyond
This ignorant present, and I feel now
The future in the instant.
Macbeth.   My dearest love,
    Duncan comes here tonight.
Lady Macbeth.   And when goes hence?
Macbeth. Tomorrow, as he purposes.
Lady Macbeth.   O, never
    Shall sun that morrow see!   60
    Your face, my Thane, is as a book where men
    May read strange matters. To beguile the time,
    Look like the time; bear welcome in your eye,
    Your hand, your tongue; look like the innocent
        flower,
    But be the serpent under't. He that's coming   65
    Must be provided for; and you shall put
    This night's great business into my dispatch;
    Which shall to all our nights and days to come
    Give solely sovereign sway and masterdom.
Macbeth. We will speak further.

62. **To beguile the time**—Deceive other people.
67. **Dispatch**—Management.

Lady Macbeth.   Only look up clear;   70
    To alter favor ever is to fear.
    Leave all the rest to me.   [*Exeunt*.

SCENE VI

Before MACBETH'S *castle. At the back are the massive stone*
    walls of the castle, encircled by a moat. The drawbridge
    is down, and the great gate stands open. The sound of
    hautboys, a kind of flute, is heard, welcoming the KING.
    Enter DUNCAN, MALCOLM, DONALBAIN, BANQUO, LENNOX,
    MACDUFF, ROSS, ANGUS, *and* ATTENDANTS.

Duncan. This castle hath a pleasant seat; the air
    Nimbly and sweetly recommends itself
    Unto our gentle senses.
Banquo.   This guest of summer,
    The temple-haunting martlet, does approve
    By his loved mansionry, that the heaven's breath   5
    Smells wooingly here;—no jutty, frieze,
    Buttress, nor coign of vantage, but this bird
    Hath made his pendent bed and procreant cradle.
    Where they most breed and haunt, I have observed
    The air is delicate.

70. **Look up clear**—Keep a pleasant face.
71. **To alter favor**—Change countenance, to show fear in your face.
 4. **Martlet**—The swallow. The passage means, the fact that the swallows
    build their nests here shows that the air is good.
 8. **Procreant cradle**—Nests where young birds are hatched and reared.

Enter LADY MACBETH.

Duncan.   See, see, our honored hostess!   10
The love that follows us sometime is our trouble,
Which still we thank as love. Herein I teach you
How you shall bid God 'ild us for your pains,
And thank us for your trouble.

Lady Macbeth.   All our service
In every point twice done and then done double   15
Were poor and single business to contend
Against those honors deep and broad wherewith
Your Majesty loads our house: for those of old,
And the late dignities heaped up to them,
We rest your hermits.

Duncan.   Where's the Thane of Cawdor?   20
We coursed him at the heels, and had a purpose
To be his purveyor; but he rides well;
And his great love, sharp as his spur, hath holp him
To his home before us. Fair and noble hostess,
We are your guest tonight.

Lady Macbeth.   Your servants ever   25
Have theirs, themselves, and what is theirs, in compt,
To make their audit at your Highness' pleasure,
Still to return your own.

Duncan.   Give me your hand;

---

13. **How you shall bid**—How you shall pray God to reward us.
14. **And thank us**—And thank me for this visit, though it cost you trouble.
20. **Hermits**—Those who pray for you.
21. **Coursed him**—Followed him.
22. **Purveyor**—Advance courier sent to provide food for the royal party.

Conduct me to mine host. We love him highly,
And shall continue our graces towards him.   30
By your leave, hostess.   [*Exeunt.*

SCENE VII

The scene is a room in MACBETH'S *castle, as in Scene V. .It
is night. In the adjoining room the banquet is going on;
servants pass through bearing dishes and flagons of wine.
As the door is opened, the noise of the feast is heard. The
door closes; all is silent for a moment, then* MACBETH
*enters. His face and manner show that he is shaken by
a mental conflict.*

Macbeth. If it were done when 't is done, then 't were well
It were done quickly: if the assassination
Could trammel up the consequence, and catch,
With his surcease, success; that but this blow
Might be the be-all and the end-all-here,   5
But here, upon this bank and shoal of time,
We'll jump the life to come. But in these cases
We still have judgment here, that we but teach
Bloody instructions, which, being taught, return

31. **By your leave**—The king courteously leads Lady Macbeth within.
 1. **If it were done**—If the murder were over with, once it is committed.
 3. **Trammel up**—Entangle.
 5. **If it were done**—If there were to be no bad consequences here and
    now, Macbeth would risk punishment in the next world.

To plague the inventor: this even-handed justice   10
Commends the ingredients of our poison'd chalice
To our own lips. He 's here in double trust:
First, as I am his kinsman and his subject,
Strong both against the deed; then, as his host,
Who should against his murderer shut the door,   15
Not bear the knife myself. Besides, this Duncan
Hath borne his faculties so meek, hath been
So clear in his great office, that his virtues
Will plead like angels, trumpet-tongued, against
The deep damnation of his taking-off;   20
And pity, like a naked new-born babe,
Striding the blast, or heaven's cherubim, horsed
Upon the sightless couriers of the air,
Shall blow the horrid deed in every eye,
That tears shall drown the wind. I have no spur   25
To prick the sides of my intent, but only
Vaulting ambition, which o'erleaps itself   — tragic flaw
And falls on th' other.

Enter LADY MACBETH.

How now! what news?

Lady Macbeth. He has almost supped; why have you left
    the chamber?

11. **Chalice**—Cup.
17. **Faculties**—Royal powers.
25. **I have no spur**—Macbeth compares himself to a rider who has no
    spurs to prick his horse, but in vaulting into the saddle, leaps too far
    and falls on the other side of his horse.

Macbeth. Hath he asked for me?

Lady Macbeth.   Know you not he has?   30

Macbeth. We will proceed no further in this business.
    He hath honored me of late; and I have bought
    Golden opinions from all sorts of people,
    Which would be worn now in their newest gloss,
    Not cast aside so soon.

Lady Macbeth.   Was the hope drunk   35
    Wherein you dressed yourself? Hath it slept since?
    And wakes it now, to look so green and pale
    At what it did so freely? From this time
    Such I account thy love. Art thou afeard
    To be the same in thine own act and valor   40
    As thou art in desire? Wouldst thou have that
    Which thou esteem'st the ornament of life,
    And live a coward in thine own esteem,
    Letting "I dare not" wait upon "I would,"
    Like the poor cat i' the adage?

Macbeth.   Prithee, peace: 45
    I dare do all that may become a man;
    Who dares do more is none.

Lady Macbeth.   What beast was't, then,
    That made you break this enterprise to me?
    When you durst do it, then you were a man;
    And, to be more than what you were, you would   50

---

32. **Bought**—Won.
37. **Green and pale**—Sickly.
44. **The poor cat**—Refers to a proverb. The cat would eat fish, but
    would not wet her feet.

Be so much more the man. Nor time nor place
Did then adhere, and yet you would make both;
They have made themselves, and that their fitness
    now
Does unmake you. I have given suck, and know
How tender 't is to love the babe that milks me;   55
I would, while it was smiling in my face,
Have pluck'd my nipple from his boneless gums,
And dash'd the brains out, had I so sworn as you
Have done to this.

Macbeth.   If we should fail?

Lady Macbeth.   We fail!

But screw your courage to the sticking-place,   60
And we'll not fail. When Duncan is asleep—
Whereto the rather shall his day's hard journey
Soundly invite him—his two chamberlains
Will I with wine and wassail so convince,
That memory, the warder of the brain,   65
Shall be a fume, and the receipt of reason
A limbeck only. When in swinish sleep
Their drenched natures lie as in a death,
What cannot you and I perform upon
The unguarded Duncan? What not put upon   70
His spongy officers, who shall bear the guilt

52. **Adhere**—Suit your purpose.
62. **Rather**—Earlier.
64. **Wassail**—Ale mixed with wine.
64. **Convince**—Overcome.
71. **Spongy officers**—Those who absorb liquor like a sponge.

Of our great quell?

Macbeth.   Bring forth men-children only;
For thy undaunted mettle should compose
Nothing but males. Will it not be received,
When we have marked with blood those sleepy two   75
Of his own chamber and used their very daggers,
That they have done 't?

Lady Macbeth.   Who dares receive it other,
As we shall make our griefs and clamor roar
Upon his death?

Macbeth.   I am settled, and bend up
Each corporal agent to this terrible feat.   80
Away, and mock the time with fairest show;
False face must hide what the false heart doth know.

[Exeunt.

72. **Quell**—Killing.
80. **Each corporal agent**—Each bodily power.

appearances against reality

"I HAVE DONE THE DEED!"
FROM THE TV PRODUCTION

ACT SECOND

Scene I

*Inverness. The castle is built in the form of a hollow square,
with a large courtyard. The* King's *sleeping apartments
were in one part of the castle;* Banquo *and* Fleance *were
lodged in another part;* Macduff *and* Lennox *were quar-
tered outside the castle. As the scene opens,* Banquo *and*
Fleance *enter and start across the courtyard.* Fleance
goes ahead, carrying a torch.

Banquo. How goes the night, boy?
Fleance. The moon is down; I have not heard the clock.
Banquo. And she goes down at twelve.
Fleance.   I take't, 'tis later, sir.
Banquo. Hold, take my sword.—There's husbandry in
      heaven;
      Their candles are all out.—Take thee that, too.   5
      A heavy summons lies like lead upon me,
      And yet I would not sleep. Merciful powers,
      Restrain in me the cursed thoughts that nature
      Gives way to in repose!
            Enter Macbeth, *and a* Servant *with a torch.*
                        Give me my sword.—   10
      Who's there?

4. **Husbandry**—Thrift.
5. **Take thee that**—Hands his dagger to Fleance.

Macbeth. A friend.

Banquo. What, sir, not yet at rest? The King's abed;
    He hath been in unusual pleasure, and
    Sent forth great largess to your offices.
    This diamond he greets your wife withal,   15
    By the name of most kind hostess; and shut up
    In measureless content.

Macbeth.   Being unprepared,
    Our will became the servant to defect,
    Which else should free have wrought.

Banquo.   All's well.
    I dreamt last night of the three weird Sisters;   20
    To you they have showed some truth.

Macbeth.   I think not of them;
    Yet, when we can entreat an hour to serve,
    We would spend it in some words upon that business,
    If you would grant the time.

Banquo.   At your kind'st leisure.

Macbeth. If you shall cleave to my consent, when 't is,   25
    It shall make honor for you.

Banquo.   So I lose none
    In seeking to augment it, but still keep
    My bosom franchis'd and allegiance clear,

---

14. **Largess to your offices**—Royal gifts to the servants.
16. **Shut up**—Ended the day.
18. **Our will, etc.**—On such short notice, we could not do all we wished.
25. **If you shall, etc.**—If you join my party, when it is formed.
28. **My bosom franchised**—My heart free (from evil).

　　I shall be counsell'd.

Macbeth.　　　　　　　　Good repose the while!

Banquo. Thanks, sir; the like to you!　　　　　　　　30

　　　　　　　　　　　[*Exeunt* Banquo *and* Fleance.

Macbeth. Go bid thy mistress, when my drink is ready,
　　She strike upon the bell.　Get thee to bed.

　　　　　　　　　　　　　[*Exit* Servant.

　　Is this a dagger which I see before me,
　　The handle toward my hand?　Come, let me clutch
　　　　thee.
　　I have thee not, and yet I see thee still.　　　　　35
　　Art thou not, fatal vision, sensible
　　To feeling as to sight? or art thou but
　　A dagger of the mind, a false creation,
　　Proceeding from the heat-oppressèd brain?
　　I see thee yet, in form as palpable　　　　　　40
　　As this which now I draw.
　　Thou marshall'st me the way that I was going;
　　And such an instrument I was to use.
　　Mine eyes are made the fools o' th' other senses,
　　Or else worth all the rest.　I see thee still;　　　45
　　And on thy blade and dudgeon gouts of blood,
　　Which was not so before.　There's no such thing!
　　It is the bloody business which informs

36. **Sensible**—Perceptible to the senses.
40. **Palpable**—Real.
42. **Marshall'st**—Leadest, as a marshal leads a procession.
46. **Dudgeon**—Handle.
48. **Informs**—Takes form.

Thus to mine eyes.—Now o'er the one half world
Nature seems dead, and wicked dreams abuse   50
The curtained sleep; witchcraft celebrates
Pale Hecate's offerings, and withered murder,
Alarumed by his sentinel, the wolf,
Whose howl's his watch, thus with his stealthy pace,
With Tarquin's ravishing strides, toward his design 55
Moves like a ghost. Thou sure and firm-set earth,
Hear not my steps, which way they walk, for fear
Thy very stones prate of my whereabout,
And take the present horror from the time,
Which now suits with it. Whiles I threat, he lives; 60
Words to the heat of deeds too cold breath gives.

                              [*A bell rings.*

I go, and it is done; the bell invites me.
Hear it not, Duncan; for it is a knell —death bell
That summons thee to heaven or to hell.   [*Exit.*

50. **Abuse**—Deceive.
52. **Hecate**—Goddess of magic.
54. **Whose howl's his watch**—Who marks the periods of the night by
    howling, as a watchman would cry the hours.
55. **Tarquin**—A Roman prince who ravished Lucretia.

Scene II

A room in the castle, the same as in Act I, Scene V. Lady
Macbeth *enters. As she speaks the opening lines, the
hoot of an owl is heard; she starts at the sound.*

Lady Macbeth. That which hath made them drunk hath
      made me bold;
  What hath quench'd them hath given me fire.
  —Hark! Peace!
  It was the owl that shriek'd, the fatal bellman,
  Which gives the stern'st good-night. He is about it;
  The doors are open; and the surfeited grooms   5
  Do mock their charge with snores: I have drugged
      their possets,
  That death and nature do contend about them,
  Whether they live or die.
Macbeth. [*Within*]   Who's there? what, ho!
Lady Macbeth. Alack, I am afraid they have awaked,
  And 'tis not done. Th' attempt and not the deed   10
  Confounds us. Hark! I laid their daggers ready;
  He could not miss 'em. Had he not resembled
  My father as he slept, I had done't.—

3. **Bellman**—The bellman, or town crier, formerly announced deaths.
5. **Surfeited grooms**—Drunken servants.
6. **Possets**—A drink made of hot milk and ale.
7. **That**—So that.

Enter MACBETH.

My husband.

Macbeth. I have done the deed. Didst thou not hear a
      noise?

Lady Macbeth. I heard the owl scream and the crickets
      cry.   15

Did not you speak?

Macbeth.   When?

Lady Macbeth.   Now.

Macbeth.   As I descended?

Lady Macbeth. Aye.

Macbeth. Hark!

Who lies i' the second chamber?

Lady Macbeth.   Donalbain.

Macbeth. This is a sorry sight.   [*Looking on his hands.* 20

Lady Macbeth. A foolish thought, to say " a sorry sight."

Macbeth. There's one did laugh in's sleep, and one cried
      "Murder!"

That they did wake each other; I stood and heard
      them;

But they did say their prayers, and addressed them

Again to sleep.

Lady Macbeth.   There are two lodged together.   25

Macbeth. One cried "God bless us!" and "Amen" the
      other;

15. **Owl, crickets**—Both the owl and the cricket were supposed to fore-
      tell deaths.

As they had seen me, with these hangman's hands.
Listening their fear, I could not say "Amen,"
When they did say "God bless us!"

Lady Macbeth. Consider it not so deeply.   30

Macbeth. But wherefore could not I pronounce "Amen"?
I had most need of blessing, and "Amen"
Stuck in my throat.

Lady Macbeth.   These deeds must not be thought
After these ways: so, it will make us mad.

Macbeth. Methought I heard a voice cry "Sleep no more!   35
Macbeth does murder sleep," the innocent sleep,
Sleep that knits up the ravell'd sleave of care,
The death of each day's life, sore labor's bath,
Balm of hurt minds, great nature's second course,
Chief nourisher in life's feast,—

Lady Macbeth.   What do you mean?   40

Macbeth. Still it cried "Sleep no more!" to all the house;—
"Glamis hath murdered sleep; and therefore Cawdor
Shall sleep no more, Macbeth shall sleep no more!"

Lady Macbeth. Who was it that thus cried? Why,
worthy Thane,
You do unbend your noble strength, to think   45
So brainsickly of things. Go get some water,
And wash this filthy witness from your hand.

---

35. **Sleep no more**—Macbeth might have heard one say "God bless us,"
but not the words here given: they are like the dagger he fancied
he saw.
37. **Ravelled sleave**—Tangled silk floss.
39. **Second course**—The chief course at a dinner.

Why did you bring these daggers from the place?
They must lie there. Go carry them, and smear
The sleepy grooms with blood.
Macbeth.   I'll go no more;   50
I am afraid to think what I have done;
Look on't again I dare not.
Lady Macbeth.   Infirm of purpose!
Give me the daggers. The sleeping and the dead
Are but as pictures; 'tis the eye of childhood
That fears a painted devil. If he do bleed,   55
I'll gild the faces of the grooms withal,
For it must seem their guilt.
                    [*Exit* Lady Macbeth. *Knocking within.*
Macbeth.   Whence is that knocking?
How is't with me, when every noise appals me?
What hands are here? Ha! They pluck out mine
          eyes.
Will all great Neptune's ocean wash this blood   60
Clean from my hand? No, this my hand will rather
The multitudinous seas incarnadine,
Making the green one red.

                    Re-enter Lady Macbeth.

Lady Macbeth. My hands are of your color; but I shame
To wear a heart so white.]   [*Knock.* 65
     I hear a knocking

55. **Painted devil**—A picture of a devil.
56. **Gild**—Smear.
62. **Incarnadine**—Make crimson.

At the south entry; retire we to our chamber;
A little water clears us of this deed.
How easy is it, then!   Your constancy
Hath left you unattended.   [*Knocking within.*
  Hark! more knocking.
Get on your night-gown, lest occasion call us,   70
And show us to be watchers.   Be not lost
So poorly in your thoughts.

Macbeth. To know my deed, 't were best not know my-
        self.   [*Knocking within.*
Wake Duncan with thy knocking: I would thou
        couldst!   [*Exeunt.*

Scene III

The south entry of the castle, just inside the great gate.   A knocking is heard without; after it has gone on some time, a Porter, *half drunk, half asleep, staggers in.   He carries a lantern and a great bunch of keys.   Instead of opening the gate, he stands grumbling, amusing himself with the fancy that he is porter of the gate of hell.*

Porter. Here 's a knocking indeed!   If a man were porter of hell-gate, he should have old turning the key.   [*Knocking within*]   Knock, knock, knock!

66. **Retire we**—Let us retire.
70. **Night-gown**—Dressing gown.
2. **Old**—A slang use, much as we say "a high old time."

Who's there, i' the name of Beelzebub? Here 's a
farmer, that hanged himself on th' expectation of   5
plenty: Come in time; have napkins enow about
you; here you 'll sweat for 't. [*Knocking within*]
Knock, knock! Who 's there, in th' other devil's
name? Faith, here's an equivocator, that could
swear in both the scales against either scale; who   10
committed treason enough for God's sake, yet could
not equivocate to heaven. O, come in, equivocator.
[*Knocking within*] Knock, knock, knock! Who's
there? Faith, here 's an English tailor come hither,
for stealing out of a French hose: come in, tailor;
here you may roast your goose. [*Knocking within*]   15
Knock, knock; never at quiet! What are you? But
this place is too cold for hell. I'll devil-porter it no
further. I had thought to have let in some of all
professions, that go the primrose way to the ever-
lasting bonfire. [*Knocking within*] Anon, anon,   20
I pray you, remember the porter.   [*Opens the gate.*

Enter Macduff *and* Lennox.

Macduff. Was it so late, friend, ere you went to bed,
        That you do lie so late?

Porter. 'Faith, sir, we were carousing till the second
        cock; . . .

5. **Expectation of plenty**—Expecting great crops, hence low prices.
8. **Equivocator**—One who took an oath with a mental reservation.
14. **French hose**—Knee-breeches—very narrow.
15. **Goose**—A tailor's smoothing iron.
24. **Second cock**—Supposed to crow at three in the morning.

Macduff. I believe drink gave thee the lie last night. 25

Porter. That it did, sir, i' the very throat on me, but I
requited him for his lie, and I think, being too
strong for him, though he took up my legs sometime,
yet I made a shift to cast him.

Macduff. Is thy master stirring? 30

Enter MACBETH.

Our knocking has awaked him; here he comes.

Lennox. Good-morrow, noble sir.

Macbeth.   Good-morrow, both.

Macduff. Is the King stirring, worthy Thane?

Macbeth.   Not yet.

Macduff. He did command me to call timely on him;
I have almost slipped the hour.

Macbeth.   I'll bring you to him. 35

Macduff. I know this is a joyful trouble to you:
But yet 't is one.

Macbeth. The labor we delight in physics pain.
This is the door.

Macduff.   I'll make so bold to call,
For 't is my limited service.   *Exit* MACDUFF.

Lennox. Goes the King hence today? 40

Macbeth.   He does: he did appoint so.

Lennox. The night has been unruly: where we lay,
Our chimneys were blown down; and, as they say,

34. **Timely**—Early.
37. **Physics**—Cures.
39. **Limited**—Appointed.

Lamentings heard i' the air, strange screams of death,
And, prophesying with accents terrible   45
Of dire combustion and confused events
New hatch'd to the woful time: the obscure bird
Clamored the livelong night. Some say, the earth
Was feverous and did shake.

Macbeth.   'T was a rough night.

Lennox. My young remembrance cannot parallel   50
A fellow to it.

Enter MACDUFF.

Macduff. O horror, horror, horror! Tongue nor heart
Cannot conceive nor name thee!

Macbeth. ⎫
Lennox. ⎭   What's the matter?

Macduff. Confusion now hath made his masterpiece.
Most sacrilegious murder hath broke ope   55
The Lord's anointed temple, and stole thence
The life o' the building!

Macbeth.   What is't you say? The life?

Lennox. Mean you his Majesty?

Macduff. Approach the chamber, and destroy your sight
With a new Gorgon. Do not bid me speak;   60
See, and then speak yourselves.

[*Exit* MACBETH *and* LENNOX.

---

46. **Dire combustion**—Destructive tumult.
51. **Fellow**—One equal to it.
54. **Confusion**—Destruction.
60. **Gorgon**—A being like a woman, but with snakes for hair: it was so
    terrible to look upon that the sight turned the beholder into stone.

                            Awake, awake!
Ring the alarum-bell. Murder and treason!
Banquo and Donalbain! Malcolm! awake!
Shake off this downy sleep, death's counterfeit,
And look on death itself! Up, up, and see   65
The great doom's image! Malcolm! Banquo!
As from your graves rise up, and walk like sprites,
To countenance this horror! Ring the bell.

                                     [*Bell rings.*

              Enter LADY MACBETH.

Lady Macbeth. What's the business,
    That such a hideous trumpet calls to parley   70
    The sleepers of the house? Speak, speak!
Macduff.   O gentle Lady,
    'Tis not for you to hear what I can speak;
    The repetition, in a woman's ear,
    Would murder as it fell.—

                Enter BANQUO.

                    O Banquo, Banquo!
    Our royal master's murdered.
Lady Macbeth.   Woe, alas!   75
    What, in our house?
Banquo.   Too cruel any where.
    Dear Duff, I prithee contradict thyself,
    And say it is not so.

66. **The great doom**—The Judgment Day.
67. **Sprites**—Spirits.

Enter MACBETH *and* LENNOX, *with* ROSS.

Macbeth. Had I but died an hour before this chance,
    I had lived a blessed time; for from this instant,   80
    There's nothing serious in mortality:
    All is but toys: renown and grace is dead;
    The wine of life is drawn, and the mere lees
    Is left this vault to brag of.

Enter MALCOLM *and* DONALBAIN.

Donalbain. What is amiss?

Macbeth.   You are, and do not know 't: 85
    The spring, the head, the fountain of your blood
    Is stopped; the very source of it is stopp'd.

Macduff. Your royal father 's murder'd.

Malcolm.   O, by whom?

Lennox. Those of his chamber, as it seem'd, had done 't:
    Their hands and faces were all badged with blood: 90
    So were their daggers, which unwiped we found
    Upon their pillows;
    They stared, and were distracted; no man's life
    Was to be trusted with them.

Macbeth. Oh, yet I do repent me of my fury,   95
    That I did kill them.

Macduff.   Wherefore did you so?

81. **Mortality**—In human life.
83. **Lees**—Dregs left in the bottom of a cask of wine.
84. **Vault**—Life is spoken of as a wine-cellar; the wine is gone, only dregs remain.
90. **Badged**—Marked as with a badge.

Macbeth. Who can be wise, amazed, temperate and fu-
        rious,
    Loyal and neutral, in a moment? No man.
    The expedition of my violent love
    Outrun the pauser, reason. Here lay Duncan,   100
    His silver skin laced with his golden blood,
    And his gashed stabs looked like a breach in nature
    For ruin's wasteful entrance; there, the murderers,
    Steeped in the colors of their trade, their daggers
    Unmannerly breeched with gore.—Who could refrain, 105
    That had a heart to love, and in that heart
    Courage to make's love known?—
Lady Macbeth.   Help me hence, ho!
Macduff. Look to the lady.
Malcolm. [*Aside to Donalbain*] Why do we hold our
        tongues,
    That most may claim this argument for ours?   110
Donalbain. [*Aside to Malcolm*] What should be spoken
        here, where our fate,
    Hid in an auger-hole, may rush, and seize us?
    Let's away;
    Our tears are not yet brewed.
Malcolm. [*Aside to Donalbain*] Nor our strong sorrow
    Upon the foot of motion.
Banquo.   Look to the lady:—   115
                [LADY MACBETH *is carried out.*

99. **Expedition**—Haste.
105. **Unmannerly breeched**—The daggers were improperly covered with
    blood.

And when we have our naked frailties hid,
That suffer in exposure, let us meet,
And question this most bloody piece of work,
To know it further. Fears and scruples shake us.
In the great hand of God I stand, and thence   120
Against the undivulged pretence I fight
Of treasonous malice.

Macduff.   And so do I.
All.   So all.
Macbeth. Let's briefly put on manly readiness,
And meet i' the Hall together.
All.   Well contented.

                    [*Exeunt all but* MALCOLM *and* DONALBAIN.

Malcolm. What will you do? Let 's not consort with
          them: 125
To show an unfelt sorrow is an office
Which the false man does easy. I 'll to England.
Donalbain. To Ireland, I; our separated fortune
Shall keep us both the safer. Where we are,
[There 's daggers in men's smiles: the near in blood, 130
The nearer bloody.]
Malcolm.   This murderous shaft that 's shot
Hath not yet lighted; and our safest way
Is to avoid the aim. Therefore, to horse;
And let us not be dainty of leave-taking,

116. **Naked frailties**—Our scantily clad frail bodies.
118. **Question**—Investigate.
123. **Manly readiness**—Clothing and armor.
125. **Consort**—Keep company with.

But shift away: there 's warrant in that theft   135
Which steals itself, when there 's no mercy left.

[*Exeunt.*

Scene IV

Scotland. An open place; in the distance is Macbeth's *castle.
Enter* Ross *with an* Old Man.

Old Man. Threescore and ten I can remember well;
    Within the volume of which time I have seen
    Hours dreadful and things strange; but this sore night
    Hath trifled former knowings.

Ross.   Ah, good father,
    Thou seest, the heavens, as troubled with man's act,   5
    Threaten his bloody stage. By th' clock, 'tis day,
    And yet dark night strangles the traveling lamp.
    Is't night's predominance, or the day's shame,
    That darkness does the face of earth entomb,
    When living light should kiss it?

Old Man.   'Tis unnatural,   10
    Even like the deed that's done. On Tuesday last
    [A falcon, towering in her pride of place,
    Was by a mousing owl hawked at and killed]

135. **Warrant**—Justification.
  4. **Trifled**—Made seem like a trifle.
  7. **Traveling lamp**—The sun.
  8. **Is't night's, etc.**—Has night overcome day, or is day ashamed to appear after such an occurrence?

Ross. And Duncan's horses—a thing most strange and
   certain—
  Beauteous and swift, the minions of their race,   15
  Turned wild in nature, broke their stalls, flung out,
  Contending 'gainst obedience, as they would make
  War with mankind.
Old Man.   'Tis said they eat each other.
Ross. They did so, to the amazement of mine eyes,
  That looked upon 't. Here comes the good Macduff. 20

     Enter MACDUFF.

  How goes the world, sir, now?
Macduff.   Why, see you not?
Ross. Is 't known who did this more than bloody deed?
Macduff. Those that Macbeth hath slain.
Ross.   Alas, the day!
  What good could they pretend?
Macduff.   They were suborn'd:
  Malcolm and Donalbain, the king's two sons,   25
  Are stol'n away and fled, which puts upon them
  Suspicion of the deed.
Ross.   'Gainst nature still!
  Thriftless ambition, that wilt ravin up
  Thine own life's means!—Then 't is most like
  The sovereignty will fall upon Macbeth.   30

 15. **Minions**—Petted darlings.
 24. **Suborn'd**—Bribed.
 28. **Ravin up**—Eat up ravenously.

Macduff. He is already named, and gone to Scone
   To be invested.

Ross.   Where is Duncan's body?

Macduff. Carried to Colmekill,
   The sacred storehouse of his predecessors,
   And guardian of their bones.

Ross.   Will you to Scone?   35

Macduff. No, cousin, I 'll to Fife.

Ross.   Well, I will thither.

Macduff. Well, may you see things well done there,
      adieu!
  Lest our old robes sit easier than our new!

Ross. Farewell, father.

Old Man. God's benison go with you, and with those   40
   That would make good of bad, and friends of foes!

                                     [Exeunt.

---

31. **Scone**—The place where Scottish kings were crowned.
32. **Invested**—With the crown.
40. **Benison**—Blessing.

ACT THIRD

SCENE I

Forres. The main hall in the palace. At the back, a dais or
low platform, on which stand two great chairs, carved and
gilded, with a canopy above them. This is the throne.
On one side of the hall is a silk hanging, embroidered
with the Scottish coat of arms; on the other, arms and
armor hang against the wall. Heavy chairs are at the
sides of the room. BANQUO *enters, and looking towards*
the throne, begins to speak.

Banquo. Thou hast it now—King, Cawdor, Glamis, all,
As the weird women promised, and, I fear
Thou playedst most foully for't. Yet it was said
It should not stand in thy posterity,
But that myself should be the root and father   5
Of many kings. If there come truth from them,
As upon thee, Macbeth, their speeches shine,
Why, by the verities on thee made good,
May they not be my oracles as well,
And set me up in hope? But hush! no more.   10

Sennet sounded. Enter MACBETH, *as* KING, LADY MACBETH,
as QUEEN, LENNOX, ROSS, LORDS, LADIES, *and* ATTENDANTS

7. **Shine**—With the light of truth.
8. **Verities**—Truths.
11. **Sennet**—Notes on a trumpet announcing the approach of royalty.

Macbeth. Here's our chief guest.

Lady Macbeth.   If he had been forgotten,
  It had been as a gap in our great feast.
  And all-thing unbecoming.

Macbeth. Tonight we hold a solemn supper, sir,
  And I'll request your presence.

Banquo.   Let your Highness   15
  Command upon me; to the which my duties
  Are with a most indissoluble tie
  Forever knit.

Macbeth. Ride you this afternoon?

Banquo. Aye, my good lord.

Macbeth. We should have else desired your good advice,   20
  Which still hath been both grave and prosperous,
  In this day's council; but we'll take tomorrow.
  Is't far you ride?

Banquo. As far, my lord, as will fill up the time
  'Twixt this and supper. Go not my horse the better,   25
  I must become a borrower of the night
  For a dark hour or twain.

Macbeth.   Fail not our feast.

Banquo. My lord, I will not.

Macbeth. We hear, our bloody cousins are bestowed
  In England and in Ireland, not confessing   30

11. **Chief guest**—Indicating Banquo.
13. **All-thing**—In every way.
21. **Grave**—Weighty, wise.
25. **The better**—Better than I expect.
29. **Bestowed**—Settled.

Their cruel parricide, filling their hearers
With strange invention; but of that tomorrow,
When therewithal we shall have cause of state
Craving us jointly. Hie you to horse; adieu,
Till you return at night. Goes Fleance with you?   35
Banquo. Aye, my good lord; our time does call upon's.
Macbeth. I wish your horses swift and sure of foot;
And so I do commend you to their backs.
Farewell.—   *[Exit* Banquo.
Let every man be master of his time   40
Till seven at night; to make society
The sweeter welcome, we will keep ourself
Till supper-time alone: while then, God be with
    you!—   *[Exeunt all but* Macbeth, *and a* Servant.
Sirrah, a word with you; attend those men
Our pleasure?   45
Attendant. They are, my lord, without the Palace-gate.
Macbeth. Bring them before us.—   *[Exit* Servant.
                        To be thus is nothing;
But to be safely thus. Our fears in Banquo
Stick deep; and in his royalty of nature
Reigns that which would be feared. 'T is much he
    dares;   50
And, to that dauntless temper of his mind,

31. **Parricide**—Crime of slaying a father.
32. **Invention**—Invented stories.
44. **While then**—Until then.
44. **Sirrah**—Sir; a word generally used in speaking to an inferior.
51. **To**—In addition to.

He hath a wisdom that doth guide his valor
To act in safety. There is none but he
Whose being I do fear; and under him
My genius is rebuked; as it is said   55
Mark Antony's was by Cæsar. He chid the Sisters,
When first they put the name of King upon me,
And bade them speak to him; then prophet-like
They hailed him father to a line of kings:
Upon my head they placed a fruitless crown,   60
And put a barren sceptre in my gripe,
Thence to be wrenched with an unlineal hand,
No son of mine succeeding. If't be so,
For Banquo's issue have I filed my mind;
For them the gracious Duncan have I murdered;   65
Put rancors in the vessel of my peace
Only for them; and mine eternal jewel
Given to the common Enemy of Man,
To make them kings, the seed of Banquo kings!
Rather than so, come fate into the list,   70
And champion me to th' utterance! Who's there?

Enter Servant, *with two* Murderers.

Now go to the door, and stay there till we call.—

[*Exit* Servant.

Was it not yesterday we spoke together?

55. **Genius**—Guardian spirit.
64. **Filed, defiled**—He committed crime to make Banquo's children **kings.**
66. **Rancors**—Bitter spite.
67. **Eternal jewel**—Immortal soul.
71. **To the utterance**—To a fight to the death.

First Murderer. It was, so please your Highness.

Macbeth.   Well, then, now
   Have you considered of my speeches?—know   75
   That it was he in the times past which held you
   So under fortune, which you thought had been
   Our innocent self? This I made good to you
   In our last conference; passed in probation with you,
   How you were borne in hand, how crossed, the instru-
         ments,   80
   Who wrought with them, and all things else that
         might
   To half a soul and to a notion crazed
   Say, "Thus did Banquo."

First Murderer.   You made it known to us.

Macbeth. I did so; and went further, which is now
   Our point of second meeting. Do you find   85
   Your patience so predominant in your nature
   That you can let this go? Are you so gospelled,
   To pray for this good man and for his issue,
   Whose heavy hand hath bowed you to the grave
   And beggared yours for ever?

First Murderer.   We are men, my liege.   90

Macbeth. Ay, in the catalogue ye go for men;
   As hounds, and greyhounds, mongrels, spaniels, curs,

---

79. **Passed in probation**—Reviewed the proofs.
80. **Borne in hand**—Kept up by false promises.
80. **Crossed**—Made to fail.
87. **Gospelled**—So full of the teachings of the gospel, such a good Christian.

Shoughs, water-rugs, and demi-wolves are clept
All by the name of dogs. The valued file
Distinguishes the swift, the slow, the subtle,   95
The housekeeper, the hunter, every one
According to the gift which bounteous nature
Hath in him closed; whereby he does receive
Particular addition, from the bill
That writes them all alike; and so of men.   100
Now, if you have a station in the file,
Not i' the worst rank of manhood, say 't;
And I will put that business in your bosoms
Whose execution takes your enemy off,
Grapples you to the heart and love of us,   105
Who wear our health but sickly in his life,
Which in his death were perfect.

Second Murderer.   I am one, my liege,
Whom the vile blows and buffets of the world
Have so incensed that I am reckless what
I do to spite the world.

First Murderer.   And I another   110
So weary with disasters, tugged with fortune,
That I would set my life on any chance,
To mend it, or be rid on 't.

Macbeth.   Both of you

93. **Shoughs**—Shaggy dogs; **Water-rugs**—Water spaniels.
93. **Clept**—Called.
99. **Particular addition**—Special title.
101. **File**—The list giving values.
111. **Tugged with fortune**—Pulled down by bad luck.

Know Banquo was your enemy.

Second Murderer.   True, my lord.

Macbeth. So he is mine; and in such bloody distance,   115
    That every minute of his being thrusts
    Against my near'st of life; and though I could
    With barefaced power sweep him from my sight
    And bid my will avouch it, yet I must not,
    For certain friends that are both his and mine,   120
    Whose loves I may not drop, but wail his fall
    Who I myself struck down; and thence it is,
    That I to your assistance do make love,
    Masking the business from the common eye
    For sundry weighty reasons.

Second Murderer.   We shall, my lord,   125
    Perform what you command us.

First Murderer.   Though our lives—

Macbeth. Your spirits shine through you. Within this
       hour at most
    I will advise you where to plant yourselves,
    Acquaint you with the perfect spy o' the time,—
    The moment on't; for't must be done to-night,   130
    And something from the Palace; always thought
    That I require a clearness. And with him—
    To leave no rubs nor botches in the work—

---

115. **Distance**—The space separating those who fought a duel with swords.
119. **Avouch it**—Take the responsibility for it.
121. **But wail**—But must bewail his fall.
129. **Acquaint you, etc.**—Inform you by a spy of the exact time.
132. **That I require a clearness**—That I am to be clear of suspicion.

Fleance, his son, that keeps him company,
Whose absence is no less material to me   135
Than is his father's, must embrace the fate
Of that dark hour. Resolve yourselves apart;
I'll come to you anon.

Both Murderers.   We are resolved, my lord.

Macbeth. I'll call upon you straight; abide within.

                              [*Exeunt* Murderers.

It is concluded. Banquo, thy soul's flight,   140
If it find heaven, must find it out to-night.   [*Exit.*

Scene II

The Same.

Enter Lady Macbeth *and a* Servant.

Lady Macbeth. Is Banquo gone from court?

Servant. Ay, madam, but returns again to-night.

Lady Macbeth. Say to the King, I would attend his leisure
For a few words.

Servant.   Madam, I will.   [*Exit.*

Lady Macbeth.   Nought 's had, all 's spent,
Where our desire is got without content;   5

137. **Resolve**—Make up your minds.
139. **Straight**—Very shortly.
  3. **Attend**—Await.

'T is safer to be that which we destroy
Than by destruction dwell in doubtful joy.—

Enter MACBETH.

How now, my lord! why do you keep alone,
Of sorriest fancies your companions making;
Using those thoughts which should indeed have died   10
With them they think on? Things without all
    remedy
Should be without regard; what's done is done.
Macbeth. We have scotch'd the snake, not killed it;
She 'll close and be herself, whilst our poor malice
Remains in danger of her former tooth.   15
But let the frame of things disjoint, both the worlds
    suffer,
Ere we will eat our meal in fear, and sleep
In the affliction of these terrible dreams
That shake us nightly. Better be with the dead,
Whom we, to gain our peace, have sent to peace,   20
Than on the torture of the mind to lie
In restless ecstasy. Duncan is in his grave;
After life's fitful fever he sleeps well;
Treason has done his worst; nor steel, nor poison,
Malice domestic, foreign levy, nothing,   25

11. **Things**—Things that cannot be helped should be disregarded.
13. **Scotched**—Cut.
16. **Frame of things disjoint**—Let the world go to smash.
25. **Malice domestic**—Revolt at home.
25. **Foreign levy**--The raising of troops abroad.

Can touch him further.

Lady Macbeth.   Come on;
Gentle my lord, sleek o'er your rugged looks;
Be bright and jovial among your guests to-night.

Macbeth. So shall I, love; and so, I pray, be you.
Let your remembrance apply to Banquo;   30
Present him eminence, both with eye and tongue;
Unsafe the while, that we
Must lave our honors in these flattering streams,
And make our faces vizards to our hearts,
Disguising what they are.

Lady Macbeth.   You must leave this.   35

Macbeth. Oh, full of scorpions is my mind, dear wife!
Thou know'st that Banquo, and his Fleance, lives.

Lady Macbeth. But in them nature's copy's not eterne.

Macbeth. There's comfort yet; they are assailable;
Then be thou jocund. Ere the bat hath flown   *sent the murderers*   40
His cloistered flight, ere to black Hecate's summons   *speaks in riddles*
The shard-borne beetle with his drowsy hums
Hath rung night's yawning peal, there shall be done
A deed of dreadful note.

Lady Macbeth.   What's to be done?

Macbeth. Be innocent of the knowledge, dearest chuck,   45
Till thou applaud the deed.—Come, seeling night,

33. **Must lave**—Must keep our royal dignity clear by flattering Banquo.
38. **But in them, etc.**—They do not hold a perpetual lease on life.
41. **Hecate**—Goddess of magic.
42. **Shard-borne**—The shards are the hard wing-covers.
46. **Seeling night**—Seeling meant to close the eyes of a hawk with thread.

Scarf up the tender eye of pitiful day;
And with thy bloody and invisible hand
Cancel and tear to pieces that great bond
Which keeps me pale!—Light thickens, and the crow   50
Makes wing to th' rooky wood;
Good things of day begin to droop and drowse,
Whiles night's black agents to their preys do rouse.
Thou marvelest at my words; but hold thee still;
Things bad begun make strong themselves by ill.   55
So, prithee, go with me.   [*Exeunt.*

SCENE III

*A Park near the Palace. It is late evening, under the trees it
is already dark, a road is seen in the foreground. Three
MURDERERS enter; the third has just joined the other two,
and they are doubtful about him. A few minutes later
the tramp of horses is heard, then the voice of BANQUO,
at which the MURDERERS hide behind the trees.*

First Murderer. But who did bid thee join with us?
Third Murderer.   Macbeth.
Second Murderer. He need not our mistrust, since he de-
        livers

49. **Bond**—A legal document, here signifying Banquo's right to live.
51. **Rooky**—Gloomy.
56. **Prithee**—I pray thee.
2. **Our mistrust**—We need not mistrust him, since he knows all about
    the affair.

Our offices and what we have to do,
To the direction just.
First Murderer.   Then stand with us.—
The west yet glimmers with some streaks of day.   5
Now spurs the lated traveler apace
To gain the timely inn, and near approaches
The subject of our watch.
Third Murderer.   Hark! I hear horses.
Banquo. [*Within*] Give us a light there, ho!
Second Murderer.   Then 't is he; the rest
That are within the note of expectation   10
Already are i' the court.
First Murderer.   His horses go about.
Third Murderer. Almost a mile; but he does usually—
So all men do—from hence to th' Palace-gate
Make it their walk.

Enter BANQUO *and* FLEANCE *with a torch.*

Second Murderer.   A light, a light!
Third Murderer.   'T is he.
First Murderer. Stand to 't.   15
Banquo. It will be rain to-night.
First Murderer.   Let it come down.
                    [*They set upon* BANQUO.
Banquo. O, treachery! Fly, good Fleance, fly, fly, fly!
Thou mayst revenge. O slave!

6. **Lated**—Belated.
10. **Note of expectation**—List of expected guests.

[*Dies.* FLEANCE *escapes.*

Third Murderer. Who did strike out the light?

First Murderer. Was 't not the way?

Third Murderer. There's but one down; the son is fled.

Second Murderer. We have lost 20
Best half of our affair.

First Murderer. Well, let's away and say how much is
done. [*Exeunt.*

SCENE IV

*The scene is the great hall of the palace, as in Scene I. At the
back is the throne, with its two chairs of state. At right
and left long tables extend from back to front; dishes and
wine cups on the tables, heavy chairs at the sides. All is
ready for the coronation banquet. Enter* MACBETH *and*
LADY MACBETH, *both in royal robes, followed by* ROSS,
LENNOX *and other lords and by attendants.* MACBETH *con-
ducts* LADY MACBETH *to the throne, then he walks about
among the guests; seeing the* MURDERER *at the door, he
goes and speaks to him.*

Macbeth. You know your own degrees; sit down: at first
And last the hearty welcome.

Lords. Thanks to your Majesty.

Macbeth. Ourself will mingle with society
And play the humble host.

1. **Degrees**—Rank. The guests were seated according to rank.

Our hostess keeps her state, but in best time   5
We will require her welcome.

Lady Macbeth. Pronounce it for me, sir, to all our friends,
For my heart speaks they are welcome.

FIRST MURDERER *appears at the door.*

Macbeth. See, they encounter thee with their hearts'
   thanks.—

Both sides are even. Here I'll sit i' the midst.   10
Be large in mirth; anon we'll drink a measure
   The table round.   [*Approaching the door.*
          There's blood upon thy face.

Murderer. 'Tis Banquo's then.

Macbeth. 'Tis better thee without than he within.
Is he dispatched?   15

Murderer. My lord, his throat is cut; that I did for him.

Macbeth. Thou art the best o' the cut-throats; yet he's
   good
That did the like for Fleance. If thou didst it,
Thou art the nonpareil.

Murderer.   Most royal sir,
Fleance is 'scaped.   20

Macbeth. [*Aside*] Then comes my fit again; I had else
   been perfect,

5. **State**—Chair of state.
6. **Require**—Request.
14. **'Tis better, etc.**—It is better outside of you than inside him.
19. **Nonpareil**—Person without an equal.
21. **Fit**—Fit of horror.

Whole as the marble, founded as the rock,
As broad and general as the casing air;
But now I am cabined, cribbed, confined, bound in
To saucy doubts and fears. But Banquo 's safe?   25
Murderer. Ay, my good lord; safe in a ditch he bides,
With twenty trenchèd gashes on his head;
The least a death to nature.
Macbeth.   Thanks for that.—
     [*Aside*] There the grown serpent lies; the worm that's
          fled
Hath nature that in time will venom breed,   30
No teeth for the present.—Get thee gone; tomorrow
We 'll hear ourselves again.   [*Exit* Murderer.
Lady Macbeth.   My royal lord,
You do not give the cheer; the feast is sold
That is not often vouched, while 'tis a-making,
'Tis given with welcome. To feed were best at home; 35
From thence the sauce to meat is ceremony;
Meeting were bare without it.
Macbeth.   Sweet remembrancer!—
Now good digestion wait on appetite,
And health on both!
Lennox.   May't please your Highness sit.

23. **Casing air**—Surrounding air.
25. **Saucy**—Insolent.
27. **Trenched**—Deep-cut.
32. **Ourselves**—Each other.
33. **The cheer**—The words of welcome.

The Ghost of Banquo *enters, and sits in* Macbeth's *place.*

Macbeth. Here had we now our country's honor roofed,   40
 Were the graced person of our Banquo present;
 Who may I rather challenge for unkindness
 Than pity for mischance!
Ross.   His absence, sir,
 Lays blame upon his promise. Please't your High-
  ness
 To grace us with your royal company.   45
Macbeth. The table's full.
Lennox.   Here is a place reserved, sir.
Macbeth. Where?
Lennox. Here, my good lord. What is't that moves your
  Highness?
Macbeth. Which of you have done this?
Lords.   What, my good lord?
Macbeth. Thou canst not say I did it; never shake   50
 Thy gory locks at me.
Ross. Gentlemen, rise; his Highness is not well.
Lady Macbeth. Sit, worthy friends: my lord is often thus,
 And hath been from his youth. Pray you, keep seat;
 The fit is momentary; upon a thought   55
 He will again be well. If much you note him,
 You shall offend him and extend his passion;

40. **Roofed**—Under one roof.
46. **Here is a place reserved**—Macbeth does not see the ghost until
 Lennox points directly to the chair; the others do not see the ghost.
49. **Which of you have done this**—i.e. This murder.
55. **Upon a thought**—In a moment.

Feed, and regard him not.—Are you a man?

Macbeth. Ay, and a bold one, that dare look on that
Which might appall the devil.

Lady Macbeth. [*Aside to Macbeth*] O proper stuff!   60
This is the very painting of your fear;
This is the air-drawn dagger which, you said,
Led you to Duncan. O, these flaws and starts,
Impostors to true fear, would well become
A woman's story at a winter's fire,   65
Authorized by her grandam. Shame itself!
Why do you make such faces? When all 's done,
You look but on a stool.

Macbeth. Prithee, see there! behold! look! lo! how say
you?—
Why, what care I? If thou canst nod, speak too.—   70
If charnel-houses and our graves must send
Those that we bury back, our monuments
Shall be the maws of kites.   [*Exit* GHOST.

Lady Macbeth.   What! quite unmanned in folly?

Macbeth. If I stand here, I saw him.

Lady Macbeth. Fie, for shame!

Macbeth. Blood hath been shed ere now, i' the olden
time,   75
Ere humane statute purged the gentle weal;

58. **Are you a man?**—Spoken aside, not heard by the guests.
71. **Charnel-houses**—Vaults used for the bones of unknown dead.
73. **Maws of kites, stomachs of birds**—If graves send back their dead,
we might as well let the birds pick our bones.
76. **Ere humane**—Before laws made the common weal (state) gentle.

Ay, and since too, murders have been perform'd
Too terrible for the ear: the time has been,
That, when the brains were out, the man would die,
And there an end; but now, they rise again,   80
With twenty mortal murders on their crowns,
And push us from our stools. This is more strange
Than such a murder is.

Lady Macbeth.   My worthy lord,
Your noble friends do lack you.

Macbeth.   I do forget.—   85
Do not muse at me, my most worthy friends;
I have a strange infirmity, which is nothing
To those that know me. Come, love and health to all!
Then I'll sit down.—Give me some wine; fill full.—
I drink to the general joy o' the whole table,
And to our dear friend Banquo, whom we miss.   90
Would he were here!   To all, and him, we thirst,
And all to all!

Lords.   Our duties, and the pledge!

Enter the GHOST OF BANQUO.

Macbeth. Avaunt! and quit my sight! Let the earth hide
       thee!
Thy bones are marrowless, thy blood is cold;
Thou hast no speculation in those eyes   95

92. **Enter the Ghost**—As before, Macbeth does not see the ghost at once:
    only as he offers a toast, and turns does he see it.
93. **Avaunt!**—Begone!
95. **Speculation**—Power to see.

Which thou dost glare with!

Lady Macbeth.   Think of this, good peers,
But as a thing of custom; 'tis no other;
Only it spoils the pleasure of the time.

Macbeth. What man dare, I dare.

Approach thou like the rugged Russian bear,   100
The armed rhinoceros, or the Hyrcan tiger;
Take any shape but that, and my firm nerves
Shall never tremble. Or be alive again,
And dare me to the desert with thy sword;
If trembling I inhabit then, protest me   105
The baby of a girl. Hence, horrible shadow!
Unreal mockery, hence!   [*Exit* Ghost.
                         Why, so; being gone,
I am a man again.—Pray you, sit still.

Lady Macbeth. You have displaced the mirth, broke the
          good meeting,
With most admired disorder.

Macbeth.   Can such things be,   110
And overcome us like a summer's cloud,
Without our special wonder? You make me strange
Even to the disposition that I owe,
When now I think you can behold such sights,
And keep the natural ruby of your cheeks,   115

101. **Hyrcan, Hyrcania**—A region supposed to be full of all wild beasts.
105. **Inhabit**—Delay. **Protest**—Proclaim.
106. **Baby of a girl**—A child's doll.
110. **Admired**—Wondered at.
113. **Owe**—Own.

When mine is blanched with fear.

Ross.   What sights, my lord?

Lady Macbeth. I pray you, speak not; he grows worse and
        worse;
        Question enrages him; at once, good-night.
        Stand not upon the order of your going,
        But go at once.

Lennox.   Good-night; and better health   120
        Attend his Majesty!

Lady Macbeth.   A kind good-night to all!

        Exeunt all but Macbeth *and* Lady Macbeth.

Macbeth. It will have blood, they say; blood will have
        blood.
    Stones have been known to move and trees to speak;
        Augurs and understood relations have
        By magot-pies and choughs and rooks brought forth 125
        The secret'st man of blood. What is the night?

Lady Macbeth. Almost at odds with morning, which is
        which.

Macbeth. How say'st thou, that Macduff denies his per-
        son
        At our great bidding?

Lady Macbeth.   Did you send to him, sir?

123. **Stones**—Stones would not lie upon the corpse of a murdered man.
124. **Augurs**—Those who in Rome foretold events.
125. **Maggot-pies**—Magpies. **Choughs**—Crows.
126. **The secret'st man of blood**—The most secret murderers.
126. **What is the night?**—What time of night is it?

Macbeth. I hear it by the way; but I will send. 130
There's not a one of them but in his house
I keep a servant fee'd. I will tomorrow,
And betimes I will, to the weird sisters.
More shall they speak; for now I am bent to know,
By the worst means, the worst. For mine own good, 135
All causes shall give way; I am in blood
Stepped in so far that, should I wade no more,
Returning were as tedious as go o'er.
Strange things I have in head, that will to hand;
Which must be acted ere they may be scanned. 140

Lady Macbeth. You lack the season of all natures, sleep.

Macbeth. Come, we 'll to sleep. My strange and self-
abuse
Is the initiate fear that wants hard use;
We are yet but young in deed. [*Exeunt.*

132. **A servant fee'd**—A paid spy.
133. **Betimes**—Early.
142. **Self-abuse**—Self-deception.

Scene V

A lonely heath, the same scene as Act I, Scene I. The day is dark; thunder is heard. Enter from one side the three Witches, *from the other side,* Hecate, *dressed like them, but a superior power.*

First Witch. Why, how now, Hecate! you look angerly.

Hecate. Have I not reason, beldams as you are,
    Saucy and over-bold? How did you dare
    To trade and traffic with Macbeth
    In riddles and affairs of death;   **5**
    And I, the mistress of your charms,
    The close contriver of all harms,
    Was never called to bear my part,
    Or show the glory of our art?
    And, which is worse, all you have done   **10**
    Hath been but for a wayward son,
    Spiteful and wrathful, who, as others do,
    Loves for his own ends, not for you.
    But make amends now. Get you gone,
    And at the pit of Acheron   **15**
    Meet me i' the morning. Thither he
    Will come to know his destiny.

2. **Beldams**—Old hags.
7. **Close**—Secret.
15. **Acheron**—A river considered by the Greeks to be the entrance to the lower world. Here is the word equivalent to "hell-hole."

Your vessels and your spells provide,
Your charms and everything beside.
I am for the air; this night I'll spend   20
Unto a dismal and a fatal end;
Great business must be wrought ere noon.
Upon the corner of the moon
There hangs a vaporous drop profound;
I'll catch it ere it come to ground;   25
And that, distilled by magic sleights,
Shall raise such artificial sprites
As by the strength of their illusion
Shall draw him on to his confusion.
He shall spurn fate, scorn death, and bear   30
His hopes 'bove wisdom, grace and fear;
[And you all know security
Is mortals' chiefest enemy.]   [*Music and a song within.*
Hark! I am called; my little spirit, see,
Sits in a foggy cloud, and stays for me.   [*Exit.* 35
          [*Song within:* "Come away, come away," etc.
First Witch. Come, let 's make haste; she 'll soon be back
          again.   [*Exeunt.*

24. **Vaporous drop**—It was believed that, when enchantments were used,
    the moon would shed a sort of foam, with great magical powers.
26. **Sleights**—Arts.
29. **Confusion**—Destruction.
32. **Security**—False confidence.

Scene VI

Forres. Before the Palace. A soldier on guard at the gate.
At a little distance enter Lennox *and another* Lord; *they*
continue a conversation which had been going on; they
speak in low tones, and guardedly, not wanting to be
overheard.

Lennox. My former speeches have but hit your thoughts,
 Which can interpret further. Only, I say,
 Things have been strangely borne. The gracious
  Duncan
 Was pitied of Macbeth: marry, he was dead:
 And the right-valiant Banquo walk'd too late;   5
 Whom, you may say, if 't please you, Fleance kill'd,
 For Fleance fled: men must not walk too late.
 Who cannot want the thought how monstrous
 It was for Malcolm and for Donalbain
 To kill their gracious father? Damnèd fact!   10
 How it did grieve Macbeth! did he not straight
 In pious rage the two delinquents tear,
 That were the slaves of drink and thralls of sleep?
 Was not that nobly done? Ay, and wisely too;

1. **Hit your thoughts**—Awakened your thoughts.
3. **Strangely borne**—There have been strange doings.
5. **And the right-valiant Banquo**—Lennox's speech is full of irony.
8. **Who cannot want the thought**—Who cannot help thinking.
13. **Thralls**—Bondmen.

For 't would have anger'd any heart alive   15
To hear the men deny 't. So that, I say,
He has borne all things well; and I do think
That had he Duncan's sons under his key—
As, an't please heaven, he shall not—they should find
What 'twere to kill a father; so should Fleance.   20
But, peace! for from broad words and 'cause he failed
His presence at the tyrant's feast, I hear
Macduff lives in disgrace. Sir, can you tell
Where he bestows himself?

Lord.   The son of Duncan,
From whom this tyrant holds the due of birth,   25
Lives in the English court, and is received
Of the most pious Edward with such grace
That, the malevolence of fortune nothing
Takes from his high respect. Thither Macduff
Is gone to pray the Holy King, upon his aid   30
To wake Northumberland and warlike Siward,
That by the help of these,—with Him above
To ratify the work,—we may again
Give to our tables meat, sleep to our nights,
Free from our feasts and banquets bloody knives,   33
Do faithful homage and receive free honors;
All which we pine for now; and this report

19. **An't please**—If it please.
21. **Broad words**—Plain speaking.
21. **He failed his presence**—Failed to appear in person.
25. **Holds the due of birth**—Withholds what is due him *by* his birth.
29. **His high respect**—The respect paid him.

Hath so exasperate the King that he
Prepares for some attempt of war.

Lennox.   Sent he to Macduff?

Lord. He did; and with an absolute "Sir, not I,"   40
    The cloudy messenger turns me his back,
    And hums, as who should say, "You'll rue the time.
    That clogs me with this answer."

Lennox.   And that well might
    Advise him to a caution, to hold what distance
    His wisdom can provide. Some holy angel   45
    Fly to the court of England and unfold
    His message ere he come, that a swift blessing
    May soon return to this our suffering country
    Under a hand accursed!

Lord.   I 'll send my prayers with him!   [*Exeunt*

41. **Cloudy**—Displeased.
47. **His message**—Macduff's message. May an angel convey the news
    ahead, so that there may be a quick and favorable reply.

THE WEIRD SISTERS

AN UNUSUAL INTERPRETATION BY THE GUIGNOL THEATRE PLAYERS

ACT FOURTH

SCENE I

The entrance to a rocky cavern, extending almost across the stage. A huge cauldron, or iron pot, stands in the foreground; the flames of the fire underneath light the scene, now leaping up and showing everything clearly, now dying down so that the scene is in semi-darkness. A crash of thunder is heard, and the three WITCHES suddenly appear. After the first short speeches, the FIRST WITCH circles the cauldron, and taking various things from a pouch at her side, throws them in; after this all take hands and circle about the cauldron, chanting their rhymes. In the same manner the SECOND WITCH and THIRD WITCH go about, and throw in their horrid ingredients, while blue and green flames leap up.

First Witch. Thrice the brinded cat hath mew'd.
Second Witch. Thrice, and once the hedge-pig whined.
Third Witch. Harpier cries; " 'T is time, 't is time."
First Witch. Round about the cauldron go;

In the poisoned entrails throw.   5

2. **Hedge-pig**—Hedgehog.
3. **Harpier**—A harpy was a monster with a woman's face and body, and a bird's wings and claws. The cat, the hedgehog and the harpy were evil spirits, who attended the witches.

Toad, that under cold stone
Days and nights has thirty-one
Sweltered venom sleeping got,
Boil thou first i' the charmed pot.

All.   Double, double toil and trouble;   10
Fire burn, and cauldron bubble.

Second Witch. Fillet of a fenny snake,
In the cauldron boil and bake;
Eye of newt and toe of frog,
Wool of bat and tongue of dog,   15
Adder's fork and blind-worm's sting,
Lizard's leg and howlet's wing,
For a charm of powerful trouble,
Like a hell-broth boil and bubble.

All. Double, double toil and trouble;   20
Fire burn and cauldron bubble.

Third Witch. Scale of dragon, tooth of wolf,
Witches' mummy, maw and gulf
Of the ravined salt-sea shark,
Root of hemlock digged i' the dark,   25
Liver of blaspheming Jew,
Gall of goat, and slips of yew
Slivered in the moon's eclipse,
Nose of Turk and Tartar's lips,

12. **Fillet**—A thin slice of meat.
16. **Adder's fork**—Forked tongue.
16. **Blind-worm**—A reptile with very small eyes.
23. **Maw and gulf**—Stomach and throat.
27. **Yew**—The yew tree was associated with death.

Finger of birth-strangled babe,   30
Ditch-delivered by a drab,
Make the gruel thick and slab.
Add therto a tiger's chaudron,
For the ingredients of our cauldron.
All. Double, double toil and trouble;   35
Fire burn and cauldron bubble.
Second Witch. Cool it with a baboon's blood,
Then the charm is firm and good.

Enter HECATE *to the other three* WITCHES.

Hecate. Oh, well done! I commend your pains;
And everyone shall share i' the gains;   40
And now about the cauldron sing,
Like elves and fairies in a ring,
Enchanting all that you put in.
    [*Music and a song:* "Black spirits," etc. *Exit* HECATE.
Second Witch. By the pricking of my thumbs,
Something wicked this way comes:—   45
        Open, locks,
        Whoever knocks.

Enter MACBETH.

Macbeth. How now, you secret, black, and midnight
        hags!

31. **Drab**—Harlot.
32. **Slab**—Slimy.
33. **Chaudron**—Entrails.
44. **Pricking**—Pricking thumbs, or burning ears, were regarded as a sign
    of something about to happen.

What is 't you do?

All.   A deed without a name.

Macbeth. I conjure you, by that which you profess,   50
Howe'er you come to know it, answer me;
Though you untie the winds and let them fight
Against the churches; though the yesty waves
Confound and swallow navigation up;
Though bladed corn be lodged and trees blown down;   55
Though castles topple on their warders' heads;
Though palaces and pyramids do slope
Their heads to their foundations; though the treasure
Of nature's germins tumble all together,
Even till destruction sicken; answer me   60
To what I ask you.

First Witch.   Speak.

Second Witch.   Demand.

Third Witch.   We'll answer.

First Witch. Say, if thou 'dst rather hear it from our
mouths,
Or from our masters?

Macbeth.   Call 'em, let me see 'em.

First Witch. Pour in sow's blood, that hath eaten
Her nine farrow; grease that 's sweaten   65
From the murderer's gibbet throw

---

53. **Yesty**—Foaming like yeast.
55. **Lodged**—Blown over and tangled together.
59. **Germins**—Germs.
65. **Farrow**—Litter of pigs.
66. **Gibbet**—Scaffold.

Into the flame.

All.   Come, high or low;
Thyself and office deftly show!
    Thunder.   First Apparition: *an armed* Head.
Macbeth. Tell me, thou unknown power,—
First Witch.   He knows thy thought;
Hear his speech, but say thou naught.   70
First Apparition. Macbeth! Macbeth! Macbeth! beware
    Macduff;
Beware the Thane of Fife. Dismiss me: enough.
                                        [*Descends.*
Macbeth. Whate'er thou art, for thy good caution, thanks;
Thou hast harp'd my fear aright. But one word
    more,—
First Witch. He will not be commanded. Here 's an-
    other,   75
More potent than the first.
    Thunder.   Second Apparition: *a bloody* Child.
Second Apparition. Macbeth! Macbeth! Macbeth!
Macbeth. Had I three ears, I 'ld hear thee.
Second Apparition. Be bloody, bold and resolute: laugh to
    scorn
The power of man; for none of woman born   80
Shall harm Macbeth.   [*Descends.*
Macbeth. Then live, Macduff; what need I fear of thee?
But yet I'll make assurance double sure,

74. **Harp'd**—Struck the keynote of my fear.

And take a bond of fate; thou shalt not live;
That I may tell pale-hearted fear it lies,   85
And sleep in spite of thunder.

Thunder. Third APPARITION: *a* CHILD *crowned, with a tree
in his hand.*

What is this,
That rises like the issue of a king,
And wears upon his baby-brow the round
And top of sovereignty?

All.   Listen, but speak not to 't.

Third Apparition. Be lion-mettled, proud; and take no
care   90
Who chafes, who frets, or where conspirers are:
Macbeth shall never vanquished be, until
Great Birnam Wood to high Dunsinane Hill
Shall come against him.   [*Descends.*

Macbeth.   That will never be.
Who can impress the forest, bid the tree
Unfix his earth-bound root? Sweet bodements! good!
Rebellion's head, rise never till the wood
Of Birnam rise, and our high-placed Macbeth
Shall live the lease of nature, pay his breath
To time and mortal custom. Yet my heart   100
Throbs to know one thing: tell me, if your art

84. **Take a bond of fate**—Hold fate to its obligation.
88. **Round**—Circle, i.e., the crown.
95. **Impress**—Press into service.
96. **Bodements**—Omens.
99. **Lease of nature**—Live out his term of life.

Can tell so much: shall Banquo's issue ever
Reign in this kingdom?

All.   Seek to know no more.

Macbeth. I will be satisfied: deny me this,
And an eternal curse fall on you! Let me know.   105
Why sinks that cauldron? and what noise is this?

[*Hautboys.*

First Witch.   Show!
Second Witch.   Show!
Third Witch.   Show!
All. Show his eyes, and grieve his heart;   110
Come like shadows, so depart!

A show of eight Kings, *the last with a glass in his hand;*
Banquo's Ghost *following.*

Macbeth. Thou art too like the spirit of Banquo; down!
Thy crown does sear mine eye-balls. And thy hair,
Thou other gold-bound brow, is like the first.
A third is like the former. Filthy hags!   115
Why do you show me this? A fourth! Start, eyes!
What, will the line stretch out to the crack of doom?
Another yet! A seventh! I'll see no more;
And yet the eighth appears, who bears a glass
Which shows me many more; and some I see   120

112. **Eight Kings**—According to tradition, a descendant of Banquo was
    Walter Steward, and from Steward eight Scottish Kings were de-
    scended.
112. **A glass**—A mirror.
117. **Crack of doom**—To the Day of Judgment.

That two-fold balls and treble scepters carry.
Horrible sight! Now, I see, 'tis true;
For the blood-boltered Banquo smiles upon me,
And points at them for his. [*Apparitions vanish.*]
  What, is this so?

First Witch. Ay, sir, all this is so. But why   125
Stands Macbeth thus amazèdly?
Come, Sisters, cheer we up his sprites,
And show the best of our delights.
I 'll charm the air to give a sound,
While you perform your antic round;   130
That this great King may kindly say,
Our duties did his welcome pay.
   Music. The Witches *dance, and vanish.*

Macbeth. Where are they? Gone? Let this pernicious hour
Stand aye accursèd in the calendar!—
Come in, without there!

     Enter Lennox.

Lennox.   What 's your grace's will? 135
Macbeth. Saw you the weird Sisters?
Lennox.   No, my lord.
Macbeth. Came they not by you?

121. **Twofold balls**—James VI of Scotland was also King of England.
121. **Treble sceptres**—England, Scotland and Ireland.
122. **Now**—Said as Banquo appears, at the end of the procession.
123. **Blood-boltered**—His hair matted with blood.
135. **Stand aye accursed**—Be marked unlucky in the almanac.

Lennox.   No, indeed, my lord.

Macbeth. Infected be the air whereon they ride,
And damned all those that trust them!—I did hear
The galloping of horse. Who was 't came by?   140

Lennox. 'T is two or three, my lord, that bring you word
Macduff is fled to England.

Macbeth. Fled to England!

Lennox. Aye, my good lord.

Macbeth. [*Aside*] Time, thou anticipat'st my dread ex-
ploits:
The flighty purpose never is o'ertook   145
Unless the deed go with it. From this moment
The very firstlings of my heart shall be
The firstlings of my hand. And even now,
To crown my thoughts with acts, be it thought and
done.
The castle of Macduff I will surprise;   150
Seize upon Fife; give to the edge o' the sword
His wife, his babes, and all unfortunate souls
That trace him in his line. ⌐ No boasting like a fool;
This deed I'll do before this purpose cool.⌐
But no more sights!—Where are these gentlemen?   155
Come, bring me where they are.   [*Exeunt*

145. **Flighty**—Fleeting.

SCENE II

Fife. A room in MACDUFF'S *castle. At one side a great bed; chairs at center. Enter* LADY MACDUFF, *wringing her hands in distress, her little* SON *and* Ross *follow.*

Lady Macduff. What had **he** done, to make him fly the
      land?

Ross. You must have patience, madam.

Lady Macduff.   He had none:
    His flight was madness: when our actions do not,
    Our fears do make us traitors.

Ross.   You know not
    Whether it was his wisdom or his fear.   5

Lady Macduff. Wisdom! to leave his wife, to leave his
      babes,
    His mansion and his titles in a place
    From whence himself does fly? He loves us not;
    He wants the natural touch; for the poor wren,
    The most diminutive of birds, will fight,   10
    Her young ones in her nest, against the owl.
    All is the fear and nothing is the love;
    As little is the wisdom, where the flight
    So runs against all reason.

Ross.   My dearest coz,

---

   7. **Titles**—Possessions.
   9. **Natural touch**—Feeling of nature.
 14. **Coz**—Cousin.

I pray you, school yourself; but, for your husband,   15
He is noble, wise, judicious, and best knows
The fits o' the season. I dare not speak much
    further;
But cruel are the times, when we are traitors
And do not know ourselves; when we hold rumor
From what we fear, yet know not what we fear,   20
But float upon a wild and violent sea
Each way and move. I take my leave of you;
Shall not be long but I'll be here again;
Things at the worst will cease, or else climb upward
To what they were before. My pretty cousin,   25
Blessing upon you!

Lady Macduff. Fathered he is, and yet he's fatherless.

Ross. I am so much a fool, should I stay longer,
    It would be my disgrace and your discomfort;
    I take my leave at once.   [*Exit.*

Lady Macduff.   Sirrah, your father's dead;   30
    And what will you do now? How will you live?

Son. As birds do, mother.

Lady Macduff.   What, with worms and flies?

Son. With what I get, I mean; and so do they.

Lady Macduff. Poor bird! thou 'ldst never fear the net
    nor lime,

17. **Fits o' the season**—What fits the season.
19. **Hold rumor**—Interpret rumors in accordance with our fears.
34. **Net nor lime**—Small birds were caught in nets, or by smearing twigs
    with a sticky substance called bird-lime, or by traps.

The pitfall nor the gin.   35

Son. Why should I, mother? Poor birds they are not set
    for.

    My father is not dead, for all your saying.

Lady Macduff. Yes, he is dead; how wilt thou do for a
    father?

Son. Nay, how will you do for a husband?

Lady Macduff. Why, I can buy me twenty at any market. 40

Son. Then you'll buy 'em to sell again.

Lady Macduff. Thou speak'st with all thy wit; and yet, i'
    faith,

    With wit enough for thee.

Son. Was my father a traitor, mother?

Lady Macduff. Ay, that he was.   45

Son. What is a traitor?

Lady Macduff. Why, one that swears and lies.

Son. And be all traitors that do so?

Lady Macduff. Every one that does so is a traitor, and
    must be hanged.   50

Son. And must they all be hanged that swear and lie?

Lady Macduff. Every one.

Son. Who must hang them?

Lady Macduff. Why, the honest men.

Son. Then the liars and swearers are fools, for there are 55
    liars and swearers enow to beat the honest men
    and hang up them.

35. **Pitfall** and **gin** both mean traps.
47. **One that swears**—Swears allegiance.
56. **Enow**—Enough.

Lady Macduff. Now, God help thee, poor monkey! But
    how wilt thou do for a father?

Son. If he were dead, you'ld weep for him; if you would   60
    not, it were a good sign that I should quickly
    have a new father.

Lady Macduff. Poor prattler, how thou talk'st!

Enter a MESSENGER.

Messenger. Bless you, fair dame! I am not to you known,
    Though in your state of honor I am perfect.   65
    I doubt some danger does approach you nearly.
    If you will take a homely man's advice,
    Be not found here; hence, with your little ones.
    To fright you thus, methinks, I am too savage;
    To do worse to you were fell cruelty,   70
    Which is too nigh your person. Heaven preserve you!
    I dare abide no longer.   [*Exit.*

Lady Macduff.   Whither should I fly?
    I have done no harm. But I remember now
    I am in this earthly world; where to do harm
    Is often laudable, to do good sometime   75
    Accounted dangerous folly. Why then, alas,
    Do I put up that womanly defence,
    To say I have done no harm?

65. **State of honor I am perfect**—I know your honorable position.
70. **To do worse**—To let you be destroyed without warning.

Enter MURDERERS.

       What are these faces?

Murderer. Where is your husband?

Lady Macduff. I hope, in no place so unsanctified   80
  Where such as thou mayst find him.

Murderer.   He's a traitor.

Son. Thou liest, thou shag-haired villain!

Murderer. What, you egg!   [*Stabbing him*.
  Young fry of treachery!

Son.   He has kill'd me, mother:
  Run away, I pray you!   [*Dies*.

    [*Exit* LADY MACDUFF, *crying* "Murder!" *and*
       MURDERERS, *following her*.

SCENE III

England. Before the KING's *palace. The palace, larger and*
 more impressive than the Scottish castles, is in the back-
 ground. Before the entrance soldiers stand guard. MAL-
 COLM *and* MACDUFF *are together in the foreground, at the*
 foot of the steps that lead to the palace doors, as if just
 leaving the palace.

Malcolm. Let us seek out some desolate shade, and there
 Weep our sad bosoms empty.

Macduff.   Let us rather

 83. **Young fry of treachery**—Young offspring of a traitor.

Hold fast the mortal sword, and like good men
Bestride our down-fall'n birthdom. Each new morn
New widows howl, new orphans cry, new sorrows   5
Strike heaven on the face, that it resounds
As if it felt with Scotland, and yelled out
Like syllable of dolor.

Malcolm.   What I believe, I'll wail;
What know, believe, and what I can redress,
As I shall find the time to friend, I will.   10
What you have spoke, it may be so perchance.
This tyrant, whose sole name blisters our tongues,
Was once thought honest; you have loved him well.
He hath not touched you yet. I am young; but something
You may deserve of him through me; and wisdom   15
To offer up a weak, poor, innocent lamb
To appease an angry god.

Macduff. I am not treacherous.

Malcolm.   But Macbeth is.
A good and virtuous nature may recoil
In an imperial charge. But I shall crave your pardon; 20
That which you are my thoughts cannot transpose.
Angels are bright still, though the brightest fell;
Though all things foul would wear the brows of
          grace,

3. **Mortal**—Deadly.
4. **Bestride**—To stand over, as a soldier defending a fallen comrade.
8. **Dolor**—Grief.
10. **Time to friend**—Time favorable.
15. **And wisdom**—And it would be wisdom.

Yet grace must still look so.⌉

Macduff.　　　　　　　　I have lost my hopes.

Malcolm. Perchance even there where I did find my
　　　doubts.　　　　　　　　　　　　　　　　　　25

　　Why in that rawness left you wife and child,

　　Those precious motives, those strong knots of love,

　　Without leave-taking?　I pray you,

　　Let not my jealousies be your dishonors,

　　But mine own safeties.　You may be rightly just,　　30

　　Whatever I shall think.

Macduff.　　　　　　　Bleed, bleed, poor country!

　　Great tyranny, lay thou thy basis sure,

　　For goodness dare not check thee!　Wear thou thy
　　　wrongs;

　　The title is affeered.—Fare thee well, lord:

　　I would not be the villain that thou think'st　　　35

　　For the whole space that's in the tyrant's grasp,

　　And the rich East to boot.

Malcolm.　　　　　　　Be not offended:

　　I speak not as in absolute fear of you.

　　I think our country sinks beneath the yoke;

　　It weeps, it bleeds; and each new day a gash　　　40

　　Is added to her wounds: I think withal

　　There would be hands uplifted in my right;

　　And here from gracious England have I offer

26. **Rawness**—Precipitate haste.
29. **Jealousies**—Suspicions.
34. **Affeered**—Settled, confirmed.
43. **England**—The King of England.

Of goodly thousands. But for all this,
When I shall tread upon the tyrant's head,
Or wear it on my sword, yet my poor country   45
Shall have more vices than it had before;
More suffer and more sundry ways than ever,
By him that shall succeed.
Macduff.   What should he be?
Malcolm. It is myself I mean: in whom I know   50
All the particulars of vice so grafted
That, when they shall be opened, black Macbeth
Will seem as pure as snow, and the poor state
Esteem him as a lamb, being compared
With my confineless harms.
Macduff.   Not in the legions   55
Of horrid hell can come a devil more damned
In evils to top Macbeth.
Malcolm.   I grant him bloody,
Luxurious, avaricious, false, deceitful,
Sudden, malicious, smacking of every sin
That has a name. But there's no bottom, none,   60
In my voluptuousness. Your wives, your daughters,
Your matrons, and your maids could not fill up
The cistern of my lust and my desire.
All continent impediments would o'erbear
That did oppose my will. Better Macbeth   65

55. **Confineless**—Boundless.
58. **Luxurious**—Lascivious.
64. **Continent**—Restraining.

Than such an one to reign.

Macduff.   Boundless intemperance
In nature is a tyranny; it hath been
The untimely emptying of the happy throne
And fall of many kings. But fear not yet
To take upon you what is yours; you may   70
Convey your pleasures in a spacious plenty,
And yet seem cold, the time you may so hoodwink.
We have willing dames enough; there cannot be
That vulture in you, to devour so many
As will to greatness dedicate themselves,   75
Finding it so inclined.

Malcolm.   With this there grows
In my most ill-composed affection such
A stanchless avarice that, were I King,
I should cut off the nobles for their lands,
Desire his jewels, and this other's house: 80
And my more-having would be as a sauce
To make me hunger more, that I should forge
Quarrels unjust against the good and loyal,
Destroying them for wealth.

Macduff.   This avarice
Sticks deeper, grows with more pernicious root   85
Than summer-seeming lust; and it hath been
The sword of our slain kings: yet do not fear;

71. **Convey**—Carry on secretly.
72. **The time you may so hoodwink**—You may so blind other people
80. **His jewels**—This man's jewels.
82. **That**—So that.

Scotland hath foisons to fill up your will
Of your mere own. All these are portable,
With other graces weighed.   90

Malcolm. But I have none. The king-becoming graces,
As justice, verity, temperance, stableness,
Bounty, perseverance, mercy, lowliness,
Devotion, patience, courage, fortitude,
I have no relish of them, but abound   95
In the division of each several crime,
Acting it many ways. Nay, had I power, I should
Pour the sweet milk of concord into hell,
Uproar the universal peace, confound
All unity on earth.

Macduff.   O Scotland! Scotland!   100

Malcolm. If such a one be fit to govern, speak:
I am as I have spoken.

Macduff.   Fit to govern!
No, not to live. O nation miserable,
With an untitled tyrant bloody-sceptred,
When shalt thou see thy wholesome days again,   105
Since that the truest issue of thy throne
By his own interdiction stands accursed,
And does blaspheme his breed? The royal father
Was a most sainted king. The queen that bore thee,

88. **Foisons**—Plentiful resources.
89. **Portable**—Bearable.
99. **Uproar**—Throw into confusion.
107. **By his own**—By cutting off himself from his own rights.
108. **Blaspheme his breed**—Slander his parentage.

Oftener upon her knees than on her feet,   11(

Died every day she lived. Fare thee well!

These evils thou repeat'st upon thyself

Have banished me from Scotland. O my breast,

Thy hope ends here!

Malcolm.   Macduff, this noble passion,

Child of integrity, hath from my soul   115

Wiped the black scruples, reconciled my thoughts

To thy good truth and honor. Devilish Macbeth

By many of these trains hath sought to win me

Into his power; and modest wisdom plucks me

From over-credulous haste. But God above   120

Deal between thee and me! For even now

I put myself to thy direction, and

Unspeak mine own detraction; here abjure

The taints and blames I laid upon myself,

For strangers to my nature. I am yet   125

Unknown to woman, never was forsworn,

Scarcely have coveted what was mine own,

At no time broke my faith, would not betray

The devil to his fellow, and delight

No less in truth than life: my first false speaking   130

Was this upon myself: what I am truly

Is thine and my poor country's to command:

111. **Died every day**—Lived a life of great self-denial. Compare St. Paul's
    words, "I die daily."
116. **Black scruples**—Suspicions of Macduff's treachery.
118. **Trains**—Plots.
123. **Abjure**—Take back.

Whither, indeed, before thy here-approach,
Old Siward, with ten thousand warlike men,
Already at a point, was setting forth.   135
Now we 'll together; and the chance of goodness
Be like our warranted quarrel!   Why are you silent?
Macduff. Such welcome and unwelcome things at once
'T is hard to reconcile.

Enter an English Doctor.

Malcolm. Well; more anon.—Comes the King forth, I
  pray you?   140
Doctor. Ay, sir: there are a crew of wretched souls
That stay his cure: their malady convinces
The great assay of art; but, at his touch,
Such sanctity hath heaven given his hand,
They presently amend.
Malcolm.   I thank you, Doctor.   145
                                        [*Exit* Doctor.
Macduff. What's the disease he means?
Malcolm.   'T is call'd the evil,—
A most miraculous work in this good King,
Which often, since my here-remain in England,
I have seen him do. How he solicits heaven,
Himself best knows; but strangely-visited **people**,   150

136. **The chance of goodness, etc.**—May our chances of success be in
    proportion to the justness of our cause.
143. **The great assay of art**—The best efforts of the healing art.
146. **The evil**—Scrofula was called the King's evil, because it was believed
    that the touch of the King's hand could cure it.

All swoln and ulcerous, pitiful to the eye,
The mere despair of surgery, he cures,
Hanging a golden stamp about their necks,
Put on with holy prayers. And 'tis spoken,
To the succeeding royalty he leaves   155
The healing benediction. With this strange virtue,
He hath a heavenly gift of prophecy,
And sundry blessings hang about his throne,
That speak him full of grace.

Enter Ross.

Macduff.   See, who comes here?
Malcolm. My countryman, but yet I know him not.   160
Macduff. My ever-gentle cousin, welcome hither.
Malcolm. I know him now. Good God, betimes remove
     The means that makes us strangers!
Ross.   Sir, amen.
Macduff. Stands Scotland where it did?
Ross.   Alas, poor country!
     Almost afraid to know itself. It cannot   165
     Be called our mother, but our grave; where nothing,
     But who knows nothing, is once seen to smile;
     Where signs and groans and shrieks that rend the air
     Are made, not marked; where violent sorrow seems
     A modern ecstasy: the dead man's knell   170

152. **Mere**—Utter.
159. **Speak**—Declare.
162. **Betimes**—Early.
170. **Modern ecstasy**—A common passion.

Is there scarce asked for who; and good men's lives
Expire before the flowers in their caps,
Dying or ere they sicken.

Macduff.   O, relation
Too nice, and yet too true!

Malcolm.   What's the newest grief?

Ross. That of an hour's age doth hiss the speaker;   175
Each minute teems a new one.

Macduff.   How does my wife?

Ross. Why, well.

Macduff.   And all my children?

Ross.   Well, too.

Macduff. The tyrant has not battered at their peace?

Ross. No; they were well at peace when I did leave 'em.

Macduff. Be not a niggard of your speech: how goes 't? 180

Ross. When I came thither to transport the tidings
Which I have heavily borne, there ran a rumor
Of many worthy fellows that were out;
Which was to my belief witnessed the rather,
For that I saw the tyrant's power a-foot.   185
Now is the time of help; your eye in Scotland
Would create soldiers, make our women fight,
To doff their dire distresses.

Malcolm.   Be 't their comfort

174. **Too nice**—Too precise.
175. **Doth hiss the speaker**—People hiss at him for telling old news.
176. **Teems**—Brings forth.
183. **Out**—Under arms.
188. **Doff**—Put aside.

We are coming thither. Gracious England hath
Lent us good Siward and ten thousand men;   190
An older and a better soldier none
That Christendom gives out.

Ross.   Would I could answer
This comfort with the like! But I have words
That would be howled out in the desert air,
Where hearing should not latch them.

Macduff.   What concern they?   195
The general cause? Or is it a fee-grief
Due to some single breast?

Ross.   No mind that's honest
But in it shares some woe; though the main part
Pertains to you alone.

Macduff.   If it be mine,
Keep it not from me; quickly let me have it.   200

Ross. Let not your ears despise my tongue forever,
Which shall possess them with the heaviest sound
That ever yet they heard.

Macduff.   Hum! I guess at it.

Ross. Your castle is surprised; your wife and babes
Savagely slaughtered. To relate the manner,   205
Were, on the quarry of these murdered deer,
To add the death of you.

Malcolm.   Merciful heaven!

194. **Would be**—Ought to be.
195. **Latch**—Catch.
196. **Fee-grief**—Personal sorrow.
206. **Quarry**—A heap of slaughtered game.

What, man! ne'er pull your hat upon your brows;
Give sorrow words; the grief that does not speak
Whispers the o'erfraught heart, and bids it break. 210
Macduff. My children too?
Ross.   Wife, children, servants, all
That could be found.
Macduff.   And I must be from thence!
My wife killed too?
Ross.   I have said.
Malcolm.   Be comforted:
Let's make us medicines of our great revenge,
To cure this deadly grief.   215
Macduff. He has no children.—All my pretty ones?—
Did you say all?—O hell-kite!—All?
What, all my pretty chickens and their dam
At one fell swoop?
Malcolm. Dispute it like a man.
Macduff.   I shall do so; 220
But I must also feel it as a man;
I cannot but remember such things were,
That were most precious to me.—Did heaven look on,
And would not take their part? Sinful Macduff,
They were all struck for thee! Naught that I am, 225
Not for their own demerits, but for mine,

210. **O'erfraught**—Overburdened.
216. **He has no children**—"He" may refer to Malcolm, or to Macbeth.
217. **Hell-kite**—The kite is a bird of prey that feeds upon dead animals.
218. **Dam**—Mother.
225. **Naught**—Wicked.

Fell slaughter on their souls. Heaven rest them now!—

Malcolm. Be this the whetstone of your sword; let grief
    Convert to anger; blunt not the heart, enrage it.

Macduff. Oh, I could play the woman with mine eyes   230
    And braggart with my tongue!—But, gentle heavens,
    Cut short all intermission; front to front
    Bring thou this fiend of Scotland and myself;
    Within my sword's length set him; if he 'scape,
    Heaven forgive him, too!—

Malcolm.   This tune goes manly.   235
    Come, go we to the King; our power is ready;
    Our lack is nothing but our leave. ⌈Macbeth
    Is ripe for shaking, and the powers above
    Put on their instruments.⌉ Receive what cheer you
        may;
    ⌈The night is long that never finds the day.⌋ [*Exeunt.* 240

232. **Intermission**—Delay.
237. **Our lack, etc.**—We lack nothing but the king's permission to go.
239. **Put on their instruments**—Set to work their agents; the powers of
    heaven work through men.

ACT FIFTH

Scene I

*Dunsinane. A room in the castle. The room is large, and bare
except for a table and a chair. A door at the back opens
into* Lady Macbeth's *sleeping room. As the scene opens, a
Doctor and a* Gentlewoman, *attending upon* Lady Macbeth, *are conversing in low tones. The room is in shadow;
presently* Lady Macbeth *enters, in a white robe, her hair
unbound. She carries a taper; its light shines upon her
face, which is white and drawn; her eyes have a vacant
look.*

Doctor. I have two nights watched with you, but can per-
ceive no truth in your report. When was it she last
walked?

Gentlewoman. Since his Majesty went into the field, I   5
have seen her rise from her bed, throw her night-
gown upon her, unlock her closet, take forth paper,
fold it, write upon't, read it, afterwards seal it, and
again return to bed; yet all this while in a most fast
sleep.

Doctor. A great perturbation in nature, to receive at once   10

5. **Into the field**—Out with his army.
6. **Nightgown**—Dressing gown.
8. **Write upon't**—As if she were writing to her absent husband.

the benefit of sleep, and do the effects of watching!
In this slumbery agitation, besides her walking and
other actual performances, what, at any time, have
you heard her say?

Gentlewoman. That, sir, which I will not report after her.   15

Doctor. You may to me; and 'tis most meet you should.

Gentlewoman. Neither to you nor anyone; having no witness to confirm my speech.

Enter LADY MACBETH, *with a taper.*

Lo you, here she comes!   This is her very guise; and,
upon my life, fast asleep.   Observe her; stand close.   20

Doctor. How came she by that light?

Gentlewoman. Why, it stood by her: she has light by her
continually; 't is her command.

Doctor. You see her eyes are open.

Gentlewoman. Ay, but their sense is shut.   25

Doctor. What is it she does now?   Look how she rubs
her hands.

Gentlewoman. It is an accustomed action with her, to
seem thus washing her hands: I have known her continue in this a quarter of an hour.   30

Lady Macbeth. Yet here 's a spot.

Doctor. Hark! she speaks: I will set down what comes from
her, to satisfy my remembrance the more strongly.

11. **Watching**—Being awake.
12. **Slumbery agitation**—Moving in sleep.
19. **Guise**—Custom.
20. **Close**—Hidden.

THE SLEEP-WALKING SCENE

Lady Macbeth. Out, damned spot! out, I say!—One: two: 35
why, then, 't is time to do 't.—Hell is murky!—Fie,
my Lord, fie! a soldier, and afeard? What need we
fear who knows it, when none can call our power to
accompt?—Yet who would have thought the old man
to have had so much blood in him? 40

Doctor. Do you mark that?

Lady Macbeth. The Thane of Fife had a wife; where is
she now?—What, will these hands ne'er be clean?
—No more o' that, my lord, no more o' that: you
mar all with this starting. 45

Doctor. Go to, go to; you have known what you should
not.

Gentlewoman. She has spoke what she should not, I am
sure of that: heaven knows what she has known.

Lady Macbeth. Here's the smell of the blood still: all the
perfumes of Arabia will not sweeten this little hand.
Oh, oh, oh! 50

Doctor. What a sigh is there! The heart is sorely
charged.

Gentlewoman. I would not have such a heart in my
bosom for the dignity of the whole body.

Doctor. Well, well, well! 55

Gentlewoman. Pray God it be, sir.

---

35. **One; two**—As if counting the strokes of the clock: she is living over
in her dreams the time of Duncan's murder.
45. **You mar all with this starting**—Here she is living over again the
scene where Banquo's ghost appears.
54. **Dignity**—Rank.

Doctor. This disease is beyond my practice; yet I have
  known those which have walked in their sleep who
  have died holily in their beds.

Lady Macbeth. Wash your hands, put on your night-   60
  gown; look not so pale.—I tell you yet again, Banquo's
  buried; he cannot come out on's grave.

Doctor. Even so?

Lady Macbeth. To bed, to bed! there's knocking at the
  gate. Come, come, come, come, give me your hand
  What's done cannot be undone.—To bed, to bed, to
  bed!   [*Exit.* 65

Doctor. Will she go now to bed?

Gentlewoman. Directly.

Doctor. Foul whisperings are abroad; unnatural deeds
  Do breed unnatural troubles; infected minds   70
  To their deaf pillows will discharge their secrets.
  More needs she the divine than the physician.
  God, God forgive us all! Look after her;
  Remove from her the means of all annoyance,
  And still keep eyes upon her. So, good-night.   75
  My mind she has mated, and amazed my sight.
  I think, but dare not speak.

Gentlewoman.   Good-night, good doctor. [*Exeunt.*

62. **Even so?**—So you were guilty of Banquo's murder, too.
74. **Annoyance**—Doing herself injury; the word had a much stronger
  meaning than now.
76. **Mated**—Made helpless, as in checkmate.

SCENE II

An open stretch of country near Dunsinane. The forces opposed to MACBETH *are in two divisions, the Scotch and the English. Here we see the Scottish troops on their way to join the English. Drums are heard: enter* MENTEITH, CAITHNESS, ANGUS *and* LENNOX, *in armor, and Soldiers in Highland costume, as described in stage directions to Act I, Scene 2.*

Menteith. The English power is near, led on by Malcolm,
 His uncle Siward, and the good Macduff.
 Revenges burn in them: for their dear causes
 Would to the bleeding and the grim alarm,
 Excite the mortifièd man.
Angus.   Near Birnam wood   5
 Shall we well meet them; that way are they coming.
Caithness. Who knows if Donalbain be with his brother?
Lennox. For certain, sir, he is not: I have a file
 Of all the gentry: there is Siward's son,
 And many unrough youths, that even now   10
 Protest their first of manhood.
Menteith.   What does the tyrant?
Caithness. Great Dunsinane he strongly fortifies:

 3. **Dear**—Affecting them deeply.
 5. **Mortified**—Almost dead.
10. **Unrough**—Smooth-faced.

Some say he 's mad; others that lesser hate him
Do call it valiant fury; but, for certain,
He cannot buckle his distempered cause   15
Within the belt of rule.

Angus.   ⌐Now does he feel
His secret murders sticking on his hands;⌐
Now minutely revolts upbraid his faith-breach;
Those he commands move only in command,
Nothing in love; now does he feel his title   20
Hang loose about him, like a giant's robe
Upon a dwarfish thief.

Menteith.   ⌐Who then shall blame
His pestered senses to recoil and start,
When all that is within him does condemn
Itself for being there?⌐

Caithness.   Well, march we on,   25
To give obedience where 'tis truly owed.
Meet we the medicine of the sickly weal,
And with him pour we in our country's purge
Each drop of us.

Lennox.   Or so much as it needs,
To dew the sovereign flower and drown the weeds.   30
Make we our march towards Birnam.

                              [*Exeunt, marching.*

15. **He cannot buckle, etc.**—He cannot guide his affairs rightly.
18. **Minutely**—Every minute.
23. **To recoil**—For recoiling.
27. **The medicine of the sickly**—The man who can cure the sick state
28. **Purge**—Cleansing.

SCENE III

Dunsinane. The main hall in the castle; doors to right and left; heavy chairs at side; the walls of stone, windows small and high; a great fireplace at rear; weapons hanging on the walls. Enter MACBETH, DOCTOR, *and* ATTENDANTS. MACBETH *is greatly excited.*

Macbeth. Bring me no more reports; let them fly all:
    Till Birnam wood remove to Dunsinane,
    I cannot taint with fear. What's the boy Malcolm?
    Was he not born of woman? The spirits that know
    All mortal consequences have pronounced me thus: 5
    "Fear not, Macbeth; no man that's born of woman
    Shall e'er have power upon thee." Then fly, false Thanes,
    And mingle with the English epicures:
    The mind I sway by and the heart I bear
    Shall never sag with doubt nor shake with fear.—   10
             Enter a SERVANT.
    The devil damn thee black, thou cream-faced loon!
    Where got'st thou that goose look?

Servant. There is ten thousand—

1. **Let them fly all**—Let my subjects desert if they want to.
3. **Taint**—Be infected with.
5. **All mortal consequences**—All things that are to happen to mortals.
8. **Epicures**—The Scots regarded the English as gluttons.
11. **Cream-faced loon**—Pale-faced blockhead.

Macbeth.   Geese, villain?
Servant.   Soldiers, sir.
Macbeth. Go prick thy face, and over-red thy fear,
     Thou lily-livered boy. What soldiers, patch!   15
     Death of thy soul! those linen cheeks of thine
     Are counselors to fear. What soldiers, wheyface!
Servant. The English force, so please you.
Macbeth. Take thy face hence.—   [*Exit* Servant.
                    Seyton!—I am sick at heart,
     When I behold—Seyton, I say!—this push   20
     Will cheer me ever, or disseat me now.
     I have lived long enough; my way of life
     Is fall'n into the sear, the yellow leaf;
     And that which should accompany old age,
     As honor, love, obedience, troops of friends,   25
     I must not look to have; but, in their stead,
     Curses, not loud but deep, mouth-honor, breath,
     Which the poor heart would fain deny, and dare
          not.—
     Seyton!

                    Enter Seyton.

Seyton. What 's your gracious pleasure?
Macbeth.   What news more?   30
Seyton. All is confirmed, my lord, which was reported.
Macbeth. I'll fight, till from my bones my flesh be hacked.

     15. **Lily-livered**—Cowardly.
     15. **Patch**—Fool.
     17. **Whey-face**—Pale face.

Give me my armor.

Seyton.   'Tis not needed yet.

Macbeth. I'll put it on.

    Send out more horses, skirr the country round;   35
    Hang those that talk of fear. Give me mine armor.—
    How does your patient, Doctor?

Doctor.   Not so sick, my Lord,
    As she is troubled with thick-coming fancies,
    That keep her from her rest.

Macbeth.   Cure her of that.
    Canst thou not minister to a mind diseased,   40
    Pluck from the memory a rooted sorrow,
    Raze out the written troubles of the brain,
    And with some sweet oblivious antidote
    Cleanse the stuffed bosom of that perilous stuff
    Which weighs upon the heart?

Doctor.   [Therein the patient   45
    Must minister to himself.]

Macbeth. Throw physic to the dogs; I 'll none of it.—
    Come, put mine armor on; give me my staff.
    Seyton, send out.—Doctor, the Thanes fly from me.—
    Come, sir, despatch. If thou couldst, Doctor, cast   50
    The water of my land, find her disease,
    And purge it to a sound and pristine health,

40. **Minister to a mind**—Macbeth is here presenting his own case.
42. **Raze out**—Erase.
43. **Oblivious**—Bringing oblivion.
47. **Physic**—Medicine.
50. **Cast the water**—To diagnose disease.

I would applaud thee to the very echo,
That should applaud again.—Pull 't off, I say.—
What rhubarb, senna, or what purgative drug,   55
Would scour these English hence?   Hear'st thou of
    them?

Doctor. Ay, my good lord; your royal preparation
Makes us hear something.

Macbeth.   Bring it after me.—
I will not be afraid of death and bane,
Till Birnam forest come to Dunsinane.   60

Doctor. [*Aside*] Were I from Dunsinane away and clear,
Profit again should hardly draw me here.   [*Exeunt.*

Scene IV

Country near Birnam Wood, which is seen in the distance.
Drums, and flags flying, and soldiers.   The two armies,
Scottish and English, have now united.   Enter Malcolm,
Old Siward, Young Siward, Macduff, Menteith, Caith-
ness, Angus, Lennox, Ross, *and* Soldiers, *marching.*

Malcolm. Cousins, I hope the days are near at hand
That chambers will be safe.

Menteith.   We doubt it nothing.

54. **Pull 't off, I say**—To the servant who is trying to put his armor on
    him.
59. **Bane**—Destruction.
 2. **That chambers**—Bed-chambers.

Siward. What wood is this before us?
Menteith.   The wood of Birnam.
Malcolm. Let every soldier hew him down a bough,
     And bear't before him; thereby shall we shadow   5
     The numbers of our host, and make discovery
     Err in report of us.
Soldiers.   It shall be done.
Siward. We learn no other but the confident tyrant
     Keeps still in Dunsinane, and will endure
     Our setting down before't.
Malcolm.   'Tis his main hope;   10
     For where there is advantage to be given,
     Both more and less have given him the revolt,
     And none serve with him but constrained things
     Whose hearts are absent too.
Macduff.   Let our just censures.
     Attend the true event, and put we on   15
     Industrious soldiership.
Siward.   The time approaches
     That will with due decision make us know
     What we shall say we have and what we owe.
     Thoughts speculative their unsure hopes relate,
     But certain issue strokes must arbitrate;   20
     Towards which advance the war.⌋ [*Exeunt, marching.*

 4. **Let every soldier hew him down a bough**—This stratagem was
      used when William the Conqueror attacked Dover Castle.
14. **Censures**—Judgments.
19. **Thoughts speculative, etc.**—People may guess what will happen,
      but fighting will decide it.

SCENE V

Dunsinane. The great hall of the castle, as in Scene 3. Enter
MACBETH, SEYTON, *and* SOLDIERS, *with drums and flags.*

Macbeth. Hang out our banners on the outer walls;
    The cry is still, "They come:" our castle's strength
    Will laugh a siege to scorn. Here let them lie
    Till famine and the ague eat them up.
    Were they not forced with those that should be ours,   5
    We might have met them dareful, beard to beard,
    And beat them backward home.—

                         [A cry within of women.
                         What is that noise?

Seyton. It is the cry of women, my good lord.   *[Exit.*

Macbeth. I have almost forgot the taste of fears;
    The time has been, my senses would have cooled   10
    To hear a night-shriek; and my fell of hair
    Would at a dismal treatise rouse and stir
    As life were in't. I have supped full with horrors;
    Direness, familiar to my slaughterous thoughts,
    Cannot once start me.—

  5. **Forced**—Reinforced.
 11. **Fell of hair**—Shock of hair.
 12. **Dismal treatise**—A tragic account.
 14. **Direness**—Horror.

nemesis—what he deserves

Enter SEYTON.

Wherefore was that cry?   15

Seyton. The Queen, my Lord, is dead.

Macbeth. She should have died hereafter;
There would have been a time for such a word.
Tomorrow, and tomorrow, and tomorrow,
Creeps in this petty pace from day to day,   20
To the last syllable of recorded time;
And all our yesterdays have lighted fools
The way to dusty death. Out, out, brief candle!
Life's but a walking shadow, a poor player
That struts and frets his hour upon the stage,   25
And then is heard no more: it is a tale
Told by an idiot, full of sound and fury,
Signifying nothing.—

Enter a MESSENGER.

Thou com'st to use thy tongue; thy story quickly.

Messenger. Gracious my lord.   30
I should report that which I say I saw,
But know not how to do 't.

Macbeth.   Well, say, sir.

Messenger. As I did stand my watch upon the hill,
I looked toward Birnam, and anon, methought,
The wood began to move.

Macbeth.   Liar and slave!   35

17. **She should have died hereafter**—When there would be time to
    mourn her death. Or it may mean, she would have died sometime.
23. **Brief candle**—Life.
33. **The Hill**—Of Dunsinane, on which Macbeth's castle was built.

Messenger. Let me endure your wrath, if 't be not so.
    Within this three mile may you see it coming;
    I say, a moving grove.
Macbeth.   If thou speak'st false,
    Upon the next tree shalt thou hang alive,
    Till famine cling thee. If thy speech be sooth,   40
    I care not if thou dost for me as much.—
    I pull in resolution, and begin
    To doubt th' equivocation of the fiend
    That lies like truth: "Fear not, till Birnam wood
    Do come to Dunsinane"; and now a wood   45
    Comes toward Dunsinane.—Arm, arm, and out!—
    If this which he avouches does appear,
    There is nor flying hence nor tarrying here.
    I 'gin to be a-weary of the sun,
    And wish the estate o' the world were now undone.—   50
    Ring the alarum-bell!   Blow, wind! come, wrack!
    At least we'll die with harness on our back.   [*Exeunt.*

40. **Cling thee**—Shrivel thee. **Sooth**—Truth as in soothsayer.
42. **Pull in resolution**—Slacken in resolution.
43. **Doubt th' equivocation**—To fear the fiend has spoken ambiguously.
47. **Avouches**—Asserts.
51. **Wrack**—Destruction.

Scene VI

Dunsinane. In front of the castle. Drums are heard, enter
MALCOLM, SIWARD, MACDUFF, *and their army, the soldiers*
carrying boughs.

Malcolm. Now near enough; your leavy screens throw
    down,
    And show like those you are. You, worthy uncle,
    Shall, with my cousin, your right noble son,
    Lead our first battle. Worthy Macduff and we
    Shall take upon's what else remains to do,   5
    According to our order.
Siward.   Fare you well.
    Do we but find the tyrant's power tonight,
    Let us be beaten, if we cannot fight.
Macduff. Make all our trumpets speak; give them all
    breath,
    Those clamorous harbingers of blood and death.   10
                                    [*Exeunt.*

   4. **Battle**—Division of the army.
   6. **Our order**—Our plan of battle.
   7. **Power**—Troops.
 10. **Harbingers**—Forerunners.

Scene VII

Another part of the battlefield. Drums and bugle calls, and
shouts are heard: dead and wounded soldiers are lying on
the ground. Enter Macbeth.

Macbeth. They have tied me to a stake; I cannot fly,
But, bearlike, I must fight the course. What's he
That was not born of woman?   Such a one
Am I to fear, or none.

Enter Young Siward.

Young Siward. What is thy name?
Macbeth.   Thou 'lt be afraid to hear it.   5
Young Siward. No; though thou call'st thyself a hotter
     name
  Than any is in hell.
Macbeth.   My name 's Macbeth.
Young Siward. The devil himself could not pronounce a
     title
  More hateful to mine ear.
Macbeth.   No, nor more fearful.
Young Siward. Thou liest, abhorrèd tyrant; with my
     sword   10

---

2. **Bearlike**—A reference to bear-baiting. The bear was tied to a stake,
   and a number of dogs set upon him. It was a common sport in
   Elizabethan England.
2. **What's he**—Who is he?

I 'll prove the lie thou speak'st.

> [*They fight, and* Young Siward *is slain.*

Macbeth.   Thou wast born of woman.
But swords I smile at, weapons laugh to scorn,
Brandished by man that 's of a woman born.   [*Exit.*

Alarums. Enter Macduff.

Macduff. That way the noise is.—Tyrant, show thy face!
If thou be'st slain, and with no stroke of mine,   15
My wife and children's ghosts will haunt me still.
I cannot strike at wretched kerns, whose arms
Are hired to bear their staves; either thou, Macbeth,
Or else my sword with an unbattered edge
I sheathe again undeeded. There thou shouldst be;   20
By this great clatter, one of greatest note
Seems bruited.—Let me find him, fortune!
And more I beg not.   [*Exit. Alarums.*

Enter Malcolm *and* Old Siward.

Siward. This way, my lord; the Castle's gently rendered;
The tyrant's people on both sides do fight;   25
The noble Thanes do bravely in the war;
The day almost itself professes yours,
And little is to do.

17. **Kerns**—Footsoldiers.
18. **Staves**—Spears.
22. **Bruited**—Noisily announced.
24. **Rendered**—Surrendered.

Malcolm.   We have met with foes
    That strike beside us.
Siward.   Enter, sir, the Castle.   [*Exeunt. Alarums.*

Scene VIII

Another part of the field. Enter Macbeth.

Macbeth. Why should I play the Roman fool, and die
    On mine own sword? Whiles I see lives, the gashes
    Do better upon them.

Enter Macduff.

Macduff.   Turn, hell-hound, turn!
Macbeth. Of all men else I have avoided thee!
    But get thee back; my soul is too much charged   5
    With blood of thine already.
Macduff.   I have no words:
    My voice is in my sword: thou bloodier villain
    Than terms can give thee out!   [*They fight. Alarum.*
Macbeth.   Thou losest labor.
    As easy mayst thou the intrenchant air
    With thy keen sword impress, as make me bleed.   10

29. **Strike beside us**—Join us and fight on our side.
 1. **Roman fool**—Among the Romans it was considered a heroic thing
   for a leader, when the battle was lost, to kill himself.
 9. **Intrenchant**—Not to be cut.

Let fall thy blade on vulnerable crests;
I bear a charmèd life, which must not yield
To one of woman born.

Macduff.   Despair thy charm;
And let the angel whom thou still hast served
Tell thee, Macduff was from his mother's womb   15
Untimely ripped.

Macbeth. Accursèd be that tongue that tells me so,
For it hath cow'd my better part of man!
And be these juggling fiends no more believed,
That palter with us in a double sense;   20
That keep the word of promise to our ear,
And break it to our hope. I'll not fight with thee.

Macduff. Then yield thee, coward,
And live to be the show and gaze o' the time.
We'll have thee, as our rarer monsters are,   25
Painted upon a pole, and underwrit,
"Here may you see the tyrant."

Macbeth.   I will not yield,
To kiss the ground before young Malcolm's feet,
And to be baited with the rabble's curse.
Though Birnam wood be come to Dunsinane,   30
And thou opposed, being of no woman born,
Yet I will try the last. Before my body

16. **Untimely ripped**—A surgical operation was performed at his birth,
   hence he was not born in a natural way.
20. **Palter**—Play tricks upon us.
29. **Baited**—Worried as a bear was by dogs.
32. **The last**—The truth of the last prediction.

"LAY ON MACDUFF"
FROM THE TV PRODUCTION

BIRNAM WOOD COMES TO DUNSINANE
FROM THE SCREEN PRODUCTION

I throw my warlike shield. Lay on, Macduff,
And damned be him that first cries "Hold, enough!"

            [*Exeunt, fighting. Alarums.*

Retreat. Flourish. Enter, with drum and colors, MALCOLM,
    OLD SIWARD, ROSS, *the other* THANES, *and* SOLDIERS.

Malcolm. I would the friends we miss were safe arrived.   35
Siward. Some must go off; and yet, by these I see,
    So great a day as this is cheaply bought.
Malcolm. Macduff is missing, and your noble son.
Ross. Your son, my lord, has paid a soldier's debt.
    He only lived but till he was a man;   40
    The which no sooner had his prowess confirmed
    In the unshrinking station where he fought,
    But like a man he died.
Siward.   Then he is dead?
Ross. Ay, and brought off the field. Your cause of sorrow
    Must not be measured by his worth, for then   45
    It hath no end.
Siward.   Had he his hurts before?
Ross. Ay, on the front.
Siward.   Why then, God's soldier be he!
    Had I as many sons as I have hairs,
    I would not wish them to a fairer death;
    And so his knell is knolled.
Malcolm.   He's worth more sorrow,   50

36. **Go off**—Die.
42. **Unshrinking station**—The place where he fought without shrinking.

And that I 'll spend for him.

Siward.   He 's worth no more:
    They say he parted well, and paid his score;
    And so, God be with him!   Here comes newer comfort.

       Enter Macduff, *with* Macbeth's *head*.

Macduff. Hail, king! for so thou art.   Behold, where stands
    The usurper's cursèd head: the time is free.   55
    I see thee compassed with thy Kingdom's pearl,
    That speak my salutation in their minds;
    Whose voices I desire aloud with mine—
    Hail, King of Scotland!

All.   Hail, King of Scotland!   [*Flourish.*

Malcolm. We shall not spend a large expense of time   60
    Before we reckon with your several loves,
    And make us even with you.   My Thanes and kinsmen,
    Henceforth be Earls, the first that ever Scotland
    In such an honor named.   What's more to do,
    Which would be planted newly with the time,—   65
    As calling home our exiled friends abroad
    That fled the snares of watchful tyranny;
    Producing forth the cruel ministers

52. **Paid his score**—As a traveler leaving an inn pays his bill.
55. **The time is free**—The people are free.
56. **Thy Kingdom's pearl**—The best men of thy Kingdom.
68. **Ministers**—-Agents.

Of this dead butcher and his fiendlike Queen,
Who, as 'tis thought, by self and violent hands   70
Took off her life;—this, and what needful else
That calls upon us, by the grace of Grace
We will perform in measure, time, and place.
So thanks to all at once and to each one,
Whom we invite to see us crowned at Scone.   75

[*Flourish. Exeunt omnes.*

70. **Self**—Her own.
72. **Grace of Grace**—Grace of God.

THE EMPEROR JONES

By

Eugene O'Neill

THE CHARACTERS IN THE PLAY

BRUTUS JONES, *Emperor*
HENRY SMITHERS, *a Cockney trader*
AN OLD NATIVE WOMAN
LEM, *a Native Chief*
THE SOLDIERS
THE LITTLE FORMLESS FEARS
JEFF
THE NEGRO CONVICTS
THE PRISON GUARD
THE PLANTERS
THE AUCTIONEER
THE SLAVES
THE CONGO WITCH DOCTOR
THE CROCODILE GOD

The action of the play takes place on an island in the West Indies, as yet un-self-determined by white marines. The form of native governments is, for the time being, an Empire.

THE EMPEROR JONES AS PORTRAYED IN THE SCREEN
PRODUCTION.

The Emperor Jones

SCENE ONE

The audience chamber in the palace of the EMPEROR—*a spacious, high-ceilinged room with bare, white-washed walls. The floor is of white tiles. In the rear, to the left of center, a wide archway giving out on a portico with white pillars. The palace is evidently situated on high ground, for beyond the portico nothing can be seen but a vista of distant hills, their summits crowned with thick groves of palm trees. In the right wall, center, a smaller arched doorway leading to the living quarters of the palace. The room is bare of furniture with the exception of one huge chair, made of uncut wood, which stands at center, its back to rear. This is very apparently the* EMPEROR'S *throne. It is painted a dazzling, eye-smiting scarlet. There is a brilliant orange cushion on the seat and another smaller one is placed on the floor to serve as a footstool. Strips of matting, dyed scarlet, lead from the foot of the throne to the two entrances.*

It is late afternoon, but the sunlight still blazes yellowly beyond the portico, and there is an oppressive burden of exhausting heat in the air. As the curtain rises a native

Negro Woman *sneaks in cautiously from the entrance on the right. She is very old, dressed in cheap calico, barefooted, a red bandana handkerchief covering all but a few stray wisps of white hair. A bundle bound in colored cloth is carried over her shoulder on the end of a stick. She hesitates beside the doorway, peering back as if in extreme dread of being discovered. Then she begins to glide noiselessly, a step at a time, toward the doorway in the rear. At this moment* Smithers *appears beneath the portico.*

Smithers *is a tall, stoop-shouldered man about forty. His bald head, perched on a long neck with an enormous Adam's apple, looks like an egg. The tropics have tanned his naturally pasty face with its small, sharp features to a sickly yellow, and native rum has painted his pointed nose to a startling red. His little, wash-blue eyes are red-rimmed, and dart about like a ferret's. His expression is one of unscrupulous meanness, cowardly and dangerous. His attitude toward* Jones *is that of one who will give vent to a nourished grudge against all superiority—as far as he dares. He is dressed in a worn riding suit of dirty white drill, puttees, spurs, and wears a white cork helmet. A cartridge belt with an automatic revolver is around his waist. He carries a riding whip in his hand. He sees the woman and stops to watch her suspiciously. Then, making up his mind, he steps quickly on tiptoe into the room. The woman, looking back over her shoulder continually, does not see him until it is too late. When she does,*

SMITHERS *springs forward and grabs her firmly by the*
shoulder. She struggles to get away, fiercely but silently.

Smithers. [*Tightening his grasp—roughly*] Easy! None
o' that, me birdie. You can't wriggle out now. I got
me 'ooks on yer.

Woman. [*Seeing the uselessness of struggling, gives away*
to frantic terror and sinks to the ground, embracing   5
his knees supplicatingly] No tell him! No tell him,
Mister!

Smithers. [*With great curiosity*] Tell 'im. [*Then scorn-*
fully] Oh, you mean 'is bloomin' Majesty. What's
the gaime, any 'ow? What are you sneakin' away   10
for? Been stealin' a bit, I s'pose. [*He taps her*
bundle with his riding whip significantly.]

Woman. [*Shaking her head vehemently*] No, me no steal.

Smithers. Bloody liar! But tell me what's up. There's
somethin' funny goin' on. I smelled it in the air first   15
thing I got up this mornin'. You blacks are up to
some devilment. This palace of 'is is like a bleedin'
tomb. Where's all the 'ands? [*The woman keeps*
sullenly silent. SMITHERS *raises his whip threaten-*
ingly.] Ow, yer won't, won't yer? I'll show yer   20
what's what.

Woman. [*Coweringly*] I tell, Mister. You no hit. They
go—all go. [*She makes a sweeping gesture toward*
the hills in the distance.]

Smithers. Run away—to the 'ills?   25

Woman. Yes, Mister. Him Emperor—Great Father— [*She touches her forehead to the floor with a quick, mechanical jerk.*] Him sleep after eat. Then they go—all go. Me old woman. Me left only. Now me go, too. 30

Smithers. [*His astonishment giving way to an immense mean satisfaction*] Ow! So that's the ticket! Well, I know bloody well wot's in the air—when they runs orf to the 'ills. The tom-tom 'll be thumping out there bloomin' soon. [*With extreme vindictiveness*] 35 And I'm bloody glad of it, for one! Serve 'im right! Puttin' on airs, the stinkin' nigger! 'Is Majesty! Gawd blimey! I only 'opes I'm there when they takes 'im out to shoot 'im. [*Suddenly*] 'E's still 'ere all right, ain't 'e? 40

Woman. Yes. Him sleep.

Smithers. 'E's bound to find out soon as 'e wakes up. 'E's cunnin' enough to know when 'is time's come. [*He goes to the doorway on right and whistles shrilly with his fingers in his mouth. The old woman springs to* 45 *her feet and runs out of the doorway, rear.* Smithers *goes after her, reaching for his revolver.*] Stop or I'll shoot! [*Then stopping indifferently*] Pop orf, then, if yer like, yer black cow! [*He stands in the doorway, looking after her.*] 50

Jones *enters from the right. He is a tall, powerfully-built, full-blooded negro of middle age. His features are typically negroid, yet there is something decidedly distinctive*

about his face—an underlying strength of will, a hardy,
self-reliant confidence in himself that inspires respect. His
eyes are alive with a keen, cunning intelligence. In man-
ner he is shrewd, suspicious, evasive. He wears a light-
blue uniform coat, sprayed with brass buttons, heavy gold
chevrons on his shoulders, gold braid on the collar, cuffs,
etc. His pants are bright red, with a light-blue stripe
down the side. Patent leather laced boots with brass
spurs, and a belt with a long-barreled, pearl-handled
revolver in a holster, complete his make-up. Yet there is
something not altogether ridiculous about his grandeur.
He has a way of carrying it off.

Jones. [*Not seeing anyone—greatly irritated and blinking*
sleepily—shouts] Who dare whistle dat way in my
palace? Who dare wake up de Emperor? I'll git de
hide frayled off some o' you niggers sho'!

Smithers. [*Showing himself—in a manner half-afraid and* 55
half-defiant] It was me whistled to yer. [*As* Jones
frowns angrily.] I got news for yer.

Jones. [*Putting on his suavest manner, which fails to cover*
up his contempt for the white man] Oh, it's you,
Mister Smithers. [*He sits down on his throne with* 60
easy dignity.] What news you got to tell me?

Smithers. [*Coming close to enjoy his discomfiture*] Don't
you notice nothin' funny to-day?

Jones. [*Coldly*] Funny? No, I ain't perceived nothin' of
de kind! 65

Smithers. Then you ain't so foxy as I thought you was.

Where's all your court? [*Sarcastically*] The Generals
and the Cabinet Ministers and all?

Jones. [*Imperturbably*] Where dey mostly runs to minute
I closes my eyes—drinkin' rum and talkin' big down   70
in de town. [*Sarcastically*] How come you don't
know dat? Ain't you sousin' with 'em most every day?

Smithers. [*Stung, but pretending indifference—with a
wink*] That's part of the day's work. I got ter—ain't
I—in my business?   75

Jones. [*Contemptuously*] Yo' business!

Smithers. [*Imprudently enraged*] Gawd blimey, you was
glad enough for me ter take you in on it when you
landed here first. You didn' 'ave no 'igh and mighty
airs in them days!   80

Jones. [*His hand going to his revolver like a flash—mena-
cingly*] Talk polite, white man! Talk polite, you
heah me! I'm boss heah now, is you forgettin'? [*The*
Cockney *seems about to challenge this last statement
with the facts, but something in the other's eyes holds*   85
and cows him.]

Smithers. [*In a cowardly whine*] No 'arm meant, old top.

Jones. [*Condescendingly*] I accepts yo' apology. [*Lets his
hands fall from his revolver.*] No use'n you rakin'
up ole times. What I was den is one thing. What I   90
is now's another. You didn't let me in on yo' crooked
work out o' no kind feelin' dat time. I done de dirty
work fo' you—and most o' de brain work, too, fo' dat

matter—and I was wu'th money to you, dat's de
reason.   95

Smithers. Well, blimey, I give yer a start, didn't I—when
no one else would. I wasn't afraid to hire yer like the
rest was—'count of the story about your breakin' jail
back in the States.

Jones. No, you didn't have no s'cuse to look down on 100
me fo' dat. You been in jail yo'self more'n once.

Smithers. [*Furiously*] It's a lie! [*Then trying to pass it off
by an attempt at scorn*] Garn! Who told yer that
fairy tale?

Jones. Dey's some things I ain't got to be tole. I kin see 105
'em in folks eyes. [*Then after a pause—medita-
tively*] Yes, you sho' give me a start. And it didn't
take long from date time to git dese fool woods' niggers right where I wanted dem. [*With pride*] From
stowaway to Emperor in two years! Dat's goin' 110
some!

Smithers. [*With curiosity*] And I bet you got er pile o'
money 'id safe some place.

Jones. [*With satisfaction*] I sho' has! And it's in a foreign
bank where no pusson don't ever get it out but me, no 115
matter what come. You don't s'pose I was holdin' down
dis Emperor job for de glory in it, did you? Sho'!
De fuss and glory part of it, dat's only to turn de
heads o' de low-flung bush niggers dat's here. Dey
wants de big circus show for deir money. I gives it 120

to 'em an' I gits de money. [*With a grin*] De long green, dat's me every time! [*Then rebukingly*] But you ain't got no kick agin me, Smithers. I'se paid you back all you done for me many times. Ain't I pertected you and winked at all de crooked tradin' 125 you been doin' right out in de broad day? Sho' I has —and me makin' laws to stop it at de same time! [*He chuckles.*]

Smithers. [*Grinning*] But, meanin' no 'arm, you been grabbin' right and left yourself, ain't you? Look at 130 the taxes you've put on 'em! Blimey! You've squeezed 'em dry.

Jones. [*Chuckling*] No dey ain't *all* dry yet. I'se still heah, ain't I?

Smithers. [*Smiling at his secret thought*] They're dry 135 right now, you'll find out. [*Changing the subject abruptly*] And as for me breaking laws, you've broke 'em all yerself just as fast as yer made 'em.

Jones. Ain't I de Emperor? De laws don't go for him. [*Judiciously*] You heah what I tells you, Smithers. 140 Dere's little stealin' like you does, and dere's big stealin' like I does. For de little stealin' dey gits you in jail soon or late. For de big stealin' dey makes you Emperor and puts you in de Hall o' Fame when you croaks. [*Reminiscently*] If dey's one thing I learns 145 in ten years on de Pullman ca's listenin' to de white quality talk, it's dat same fact. And when I gits a chance to use it I winds up Emperor in two years.

Smithers. [*Unable to repress the genuine admiration of
the small fry for the large*] Yes, you turned the
bleedin' trick, all right. Blimey, I never seen a bloke
'as 'ad the bloomin' luck you 'as.

Jones. [*Severely*] Luck? What you mean—luck?

Smithers. I suppose you'll say as that swank about the
silver bullet ain't luck—and that was what first got
the fool blacks on yer side the time of the revolution,
wasn't it?

Jones. [*With a laugh*] Oh, dat silver bullet! Sho' was
luck! But I makes dat luck, you heah? I loads de
dice! Yessuh! When dat murderin' nigger ole Lem
hired to kill me takes aim ten feet away and his gun
misses fire and I shoots him dead, what you heah me
say?

Smithers. You said yer'd got a charm so's no lead bullet
'd kill yer. You was so strong only a silver bullet
could kill yer, you told 'em. Blimey, wasn't that
swank for yer—and plain, fat-'eaded luck?

Jones. [*Proudly*] I got brains and I uses 'em quick. Dat
ain't luck.

Smithers. Yer knew they wasn't 'ardly liable to get no
silver bullets. And it was luck 'e didn't 'it you that
time.

Jones. [*Laughing*] And dere all dem fool bush niggers
was kneelin' down and bumpin' deir heads on de
ground like I was a miracle out o' de Bible. Oh,
Lawd, from dat time on I has dem all eatin' out of

my hand. I cracks de whip and dey jumps through.

Smithers. [*With a sniff*] Yankee bluff done it.

Jones. Ain't a man's talkin' big what makes him big— long as he makes folks believe it. Sho' I talks large 180 when I ain't got nothin' to back it up, but I ain't talkin' wild just de same. I knows I kin fool 'em—I *knows* it—and dat's backin' enough fo' my game. And ain't I got to learn deir lingo and teach some of dem English befo' I kin talk to 'em? Ain't dat 185 wuk? You ain't never learned ary word er it, Smithers, in de ten years you been heah, dough yo' knows it's money in yo' pocket tradin' wid 'em if you does. But yo' too shiftless to take de trouble.

Smithers. [*Flushing*] Never mind about me. What's 190 this I've 'eard about yer really 'avin' a silver bullet molded for yourself?

Jones. It's playin' out my bluff. I has de silver bullet molded and I tells 'em when de times comes I kills myself wid it. I tells 'em dat's 'cause I'm de on'y 195 man in de world big enuff to git me. No use'n deir tryin'. And dey falls down and bumps deir heads. [*He laughs.*] I does dat so's I kin take a walk in peace widout no jealous nigger gunnin' at me from behind de trees. 200

Smithers. [*Astonished*] Then you 'ad it made—'onest?

Jones. Sho' did. Heah she be. [*He takes out his revolver, breaks it, and takes the silver bullet out of one chamber.*] Five lead an' dis silver baby at de last

Don't she shine pretty?   [*He holds it in his hand,* 205
looking at it admiringly, as if strangely fascinated.]

Smithers. Let me see. [*Reaches out his hand for it.*]

Jones. [*Harshly*] Keep yo' hands whar dey b'long, white
man. [*He replaces it in the chamber and puts the
revolver back on his hip.*]   210

Smithers. [*Snarling*] Gawd blimey! Think I'm a bleedin'
thief, you would.

Jones. No. 'Tain't dat. I knows you'se scared to steal
from me.   On'y I ain't 'lowin' nary body to touch
dis baby.   She's my rabbit's foot.   215

Smithers. [*Sneering*] A bloomin' charm, wot? [*Venom-
ously*]   Well, you'll need all the bloody charms you
'as before long, s' 'elp me!

Jones. [*Judicially*] Oh, I'se good for six months yit 'fore
dey gits sick o' my game. Den, when I sees trouble 220
comin', I makes my get-a-way.

Smithers. Ho! You got it all planned, ain't yer?

Jones. I ain't no fool. I knows dis Emperor's time is
sho't. Dat why I make hay when de sun shine.   Was
you thinkin' I'se aimin' to hold down dis job for life? 225
No, suh!   What good is gittin' money if you stays
back in dis raggedy country?   I wants action when I
spends.   And when I sees dese niggers gittin' up deir
nerve to tu'n me out, and I'se got all de money in
sight, I resigns on de spot and beats it quick.   230

Smithers. Where to?

Jones. None o' yo' business.

Smithers. Not back to the bloody States, I'll lay my oath.

Jones. [*Suspiciously*] Why don't I? [*Then with an easy laugh*] You mean 'count of dat story 'bout me 235 breakin' from jail back dere? Dat's all talk.

Smithers. [*Skeptically*] Ho, yes!

Jones. [*Sharply*] You ain't 'sinuatin' I'se a liar, is you?

Smithers. [*Hastily*] No, Gawd strike me! I was only thinkin' o' the bloody lies you told the blacks 'ere 240 about killin' white men in the States.

Jones. [*Angered*] How comes dey're lies?

Smithers. You'd 'ave been in jail if you 'ad, wouldn't yer then? [*With venom*] And from what I've 'eard it ain't 'ealthy for a black to kill a white man in the 245 States. They burn 'em in oil, don't they?

Jones. [*With cool deadliness*] You mean lynchin' 'd scare me? Well, I tells you, Smithers, maybe I does kill one white man back dere. Maybe I does. And maybe I kills another right heah 'fore long if he don't 250 look out.

Smithers. [*Trying to force a laugh*] I was on'y spoofin' yer. Can't yer take a joke? And you was just sayin' you'd never been in jail.

Jones. [*In the same tone—slightly boastful*] Maybe I goes 255 to jail dere for gettin' in an argument wid razors ovah a crap game. Maybe I gits twenty years when dat colored man die. Maybe I gits in 'nother argument wid de prison guard who was overseer ovah us when we're walkin' de roads. Maybe he hits me wid a 260

whip an' I splits his head wid a shovel an' runs away
an' files de chain off my leg an' gits away safe. Maybe
I does all dat an' maybe I don't. It's a story I tells
you so's you knows I'se de kind of man dat if you
evah repeats one word of it, I ends yo' stealin' on dis 265
yearth mighty damn quick!

Smithers. [*Terrified*] Think I'd peach on yer? Not me!
Ain't I always been yer friend?

Jones. [*Suddenly relaxing*] Sho' you has—and you better
be.   270

Smithers. [*Recovering his composure—and with it his
malice*] And just to show yer I'm yer friend, I'll tell
yer that bit o' news I was goin' to.

Jones. Go ahead! Shoot de piece. Must be bad news from
de happy way you look.   275

Smithers. [*Warningly*] Maybe it's gettin' time for you to
resign—with that bloomin' silver bullet, wot? [*He
finishes with a mocking grin.*]

Jones. [*Puzzled*] What's dat you say? Talk plain.

Smithers. Ain't noticed any of the guards or servants 280
about the place today, I 'aven't.

Jones. [*Carelessly*] Dey're all out in de garden sleepin'
under de trees. When I sleeps, dey sneaks a sleep,
too, and I pretends I never suspicions it. All I got to
do is to ring de bell an' dey come flyin', makin' a 285
bluff dey was wukin' all de time.

Smithers. [*In the same mocking tone*] Ring the bell now
an' you'll bloody well see what I means.

Jones. [*Startled to alertness, but preserving the same care-less tone*] Sho' I rings. [*He reaches below the throne* 290 *and pulls out a big common dinner bell which is painted the same vivid scarlet as the throne. He rings this vigorously—then stops to listen. Then he goes to both doors, rings again, and looks out.*]

Smithers. [*Watching him with malicious satisfaction—* 295 *after a pause—mockingly*] The bloody ship is sinkin' an' the bleedin' rats 'as slung their 'ooks.

Jones. [*In a sudden fit of anger flings the bell clatteringly into a corner*] Low-flung, woods' niggers! [*Then catching* SMITHERS' *eye on him, he controls himself* 300 *and suddenly bursts into a low, chuckling laugh.*] Reckon I overplays my hand dis once! A man can't take de pot on a bob-tailed flush all de time. Was I sayin' I'd sit in six months mo'? Well, I'se changed my mind, den. I cashes in and resigns de job of 305 Emperor right dis minute.

Smithers. [*With real admiration*] Blimey, but you're a cool bird, and no mistake.

Jones. No use'n fussin'. When I knows de game's up I kisses it good-bye widout no long waits. Dey've all 310 run off to de hills, ain't dey?

Smithers. Yes—every bleedin' manjack of 'em.

Jones. Den de revolution is at de post. And de Emperor better git his feet smokin' up de trail. [*He starts for the door in rear.*] 315

Smithers. Goin' out to look for your 'orse? Yer won't

find any. They steals the 'orses first thing. Mine
was gone when I went for 'im this mornin'. That's
wot first give me a suspicion of wot was up.

Jones. [*Alarmed for a second, scratches his head, then* 320
    philosophically] Well, den I hoofs it. Feet, do yo'
    duty! [*He pulls out a gold watch and looks at it.*]
    Three-thuty. Sundown's at six-thuty or dereabouts.
    [*Puts his watch back—with cool confidence.*] I got
    plenty o' time to make it easy.   325

Smithers. Don't be so bloomin' sure of it. They'll be
    after you 'ot and 'eavy. Ole Lem is at the bottom o'
    this business an' 'e 'ates you like 'ell. 'E'd rather do
    for you than eat 'is dinner, 'e would!

Jones. [*Scornfully*] Dat fool no-count nigger! Does you 330
    think I'se scared o' him? I stands him on his thick
    head more'n once befo' dis, and I does it again if he
    come in my way—[*Fiercely*]. And dis time I leave
    him a dead nigger fo' sho'!

Smithers. You'll 'ave to cut through the big forest—an' 335
    these blacks 'ere can sniff and follow a trail in the
    dark like 'ounds. You'd 'ave to 'ustle to get through
    that forest in twelve hours even if you knew all the
    bloomin' trails like a native.

Jones. [*With indignant scorn*] Look-a-heah, white man! 340
    Does you think I'm a natural bo'n fool? Give me
    credit fo' havin' some sense, fo' Lawd's sake! Don't
    you s'pose I'se looked ahead and made sho' of all de
    chances? I'se gone out in dat big forest, pretendin'

to hunt so many times dat I knows it high an' low 345
like a book. I could go through on dem trails wid
my eyes shut. [*With great contempt*] Think dese
ig'nerent bush niggers dat ain't got brains enuff to
know deir own names even can catch Brutus Jones?
Huh! I s'pects not! Not on yo' life! Why, man, de 350
white men went after me wid bloodhounds where I
come from an' I jes' laughs at 'em. It's a shame to
fool dese black trash around heah, dey're so easy.
You watch me, man. I'll make dem look sick, I will.
I'll be 'cross de plain to de edge of de forest by time 355
dark comes. Once in de woods in de night, dey got
a swell chance o' findin' dis baby! Dawn to-morrow
I'll be out at de oder side and on de coast whar dat
French gunboat is stayin'. She picks me up, takes me
to the Martinique when she go dar, and dere I is safe 360
wid a mighty big bankroll in my jeans. It's easy as
rollin' off a log.

Smithers. [*Maliciously*] But s'posin' somethin' 'appens
wrong an' they do nab yer?

Jones. [*Decisively*] Dey don't. Dat's de answer. 365
Smithers. But just for argyment's sake—what'd you do?
Jones. [*Frowning*] I'se got five lead bullets in dis gun
good enuff fo' common bush niggers—an' after dat I
got de silver bullet left to cheat 'em out o' gettin' me.
Smithers. [*Jeeringly*] Ho, I was fergettin' that silver bul- 370
let. You'll bump yourself orf in style, won't yer?
Blimey!

Jones. [*Gloomily*] Yo' kin bet yo' whole roll on one thing, white man. Dis baby plays out his string to de end and when he quits, he quits wid a bang de way he 375 ought. Silver bullet ain't none too good for him when he go, dat's a fac'! [*Then shaking off his nervousness—with a confident laugh*] Sho'! What is I talkin' about? Ain't come to dat yit an' I never will —not wid trash niggers like dese yere. [*Boastfully*] 380 Silver bullet bring me luck, anyway. I kin outguess, outrun, outfight, an' outplay de whole lot o' dem all ovah de board any time o' de day er night! Yo' watch me!

From the distant hills comes the faint, steady thump of a tom-tom, low and vibrating. It starts at a rate exactly corresponding to normal pulse beat—72 to the minute— and continues at a gradually accelerating rate from this point uninterruptedly to the very end of the play.

Jones *starts at the sound; a strange look of apprehension creeps into his face for a moment as he listens. Then he asks, with an attempt to regain his most casual manner:*

What's dat drum beatin' fo'?   385
Smithers. [*With a mean grin*] For you. That means the bleedin' ceremony 'as started. I've 'eard it before and I knows.

Jones. Cer'mony? What cer'mony?

Smithers. The blacks is 'oldin' a bloody meetin', 'avin' a 390

war dance, gettin' their courage worked up b'fore
they starts after you.

Jones. Let dem! Dey'll sho' need it!

Smithers. And they're there 'oldin' their 'eathen religious
service—makin' no end of devil spells and charms to 395
'elp 'em against your silver bullet. [*He guffaws
loudly.*] Blimey, but they're balmy as 'ell.

Jones. [*A tiny bit awed and shaken in spite of himself*]
Huh! Takes more'n dat to scare dis chicken!

Smithers. [*Scenting the other's feeling—maliciously*] Ter- 400
night when it's pitch black in the forest, they'll 'ave
their pet devils and ghosts 'oundin' after you. You'll
find yer bloody 'air 'll be standin' on end before tomorrow mornin'. [*Seriously*] It's a bleedin' queer
place, that stinkin' forest, even in daylight. Yer 405
don't know what might 'appen in there, it's that rot-
ten still. Always sends the cold shivers down my
back minute I gets in it.

Jones. [*With a contemptuous sniff*] I ain't no chicken-
liver like you is. Trees an' me, we's friends, an' dar's 410
a full moon comin' bring me light. And let dem po'
niggers make all de fool spells dey'se a min' to. Does
yo' s'pect I'se silly enuff to b'lieve in ghosts an' ha'nts
an' all dat ole woman's talk? G'long, white man!
You ain't talkin' to me. [*With a chuckle*] Doesn't 415
you know dey's got to do wid a man who was member in good standin' o' de Baptist Church. Sho' I was
dat when I was porter on de Pullman, an' befo' I gits

into my little trouble. Let dem try deir heathen
tricks. De Baptist Church done pertect me an' land 420
dem all in hell. [*Then with more confident satisfac-
faction*] An' I'se got little silver bullet o' my own,
don't forgit.

Smithers. Ho! You 'aven't give much 'eed to your Baptist Church since you been down 'ere. I've 'eard 425
myself you 'ad turned yer coat an' was takin' up with
their blarsted witch-doctors, or whatever the 'ell yer
calls the swine.

Jones. [*Vehemently*] I pretends to! Sho' I pretends!
Dat's part o' my game from de fust. If I finds out 430
dem niggers believes dat black is white, den I yells it
out louder 'n deir loudest. It don't git me nothin'
to do missionary work for de Baptist Church. I'se
after de coin, an' I lays my God on de shelf for de
time bein'. [*Stops abruptly to look at his watch—* 435
alertly.] But I ain't got de time to waste no mo'e
fool talk wid you. I'se gwine away from heah dis
secon'. [*He reaches in under the throne and pulls
out an expensive Panama hat with a bright multi-
colored band and sets it jauntily on his head.*] So 440
long, white man! [*With a grin*] See you 'n jail some
time, maybe!

Smithers. Not me, you won't. Well, I wouldn't be in yer
bloody boots for no bloomin' money, but 'ere's wishin'
yer luck just the same.   445

Jones. [*Contemptuously*] You're de frightenedest man

evah I see! I tells you I'se safe 's'f I was in New York City. It take dem niggers from now to dark to git up de nerve to start somethin'. By dat time I'se got a head start dey never kotch up wid. 450

Smithers. [*Maliciously*] Give my regards to any ghosts yer meets up with.

Jones. [*Grinning*] If dat ghost got money, I'll tell him never ha'nt you less'n he wants to lose it.

Smithers. [*Flattered*] Garn! [*Then curiously*] Ain't yer 455 takin' no luggage with yer?

Jones. I travels light when I wants to move fast. And I got tinned grub buried on de edge o' de forest. [*Boastfully*] Now say dat I don't look ahead an' use my brains! [*With a wide, liberal gesture*] I will all dats 460 left in de palace to you an' you better grab all you kin sneak away wid befo' dey gits here.

Smithers. [*Gratefully*] Righto—and thanks ter yer. [*As* JONES *walks toward the door in rear—cautioningly*] Say! Look 'ere, you ain't goin' out that way, are yer? 465

Jones. Does you think I'd slink out de back door like a common nigger? I'se Emperor yit, ain't I? And de Emperor Jones leaves de way he comes, and dat black trash don't dare stop him—not yit, leastways. [*He stops for a moment in the doorway, listening to the* 470 *far-off but insistent beat of the tom-tom.*] Listen to dat roll-call, will yo'? Must be mighty big drum carry dat far. [*Then with a laugh*] Well, if dey ain't no whole brass band to see me off, I sho' got de drum

part of it. So long, white man. [*He puts his hands* 475
*in his pockets and with studied carelessness, whistling
a tune, he saunters out of the doorway and off to the
left.*]

Smithers. [*Looks after him with a puzzled admiration*]
'E's got 'is bloomin' nerve with 'im, s'elp me! [*Then* 480
angrily] Ho—the bleedin' nigger—puttin' on 'is
bloody airs! I 'opes they nabs 'im an' gives 'im what's
what! [*Then putting business before the pleasure of
his thought, looking around him with cupidity.*] A
bloke ought to find a 'ole lot in this palace that 'd go 485
for a bit of cash. Let's take a look, 'Arry, me lad.
[*He starts for the doorway on right as the curtain
falls.*]

SCENE TWO

*Nightfall. The end of the plain where the Great Forest
begins. The foreground is sandy, level ground, dotted
by a few stones and clumps of stunted bushes cowering
close against the earth to escape the buffeting of the trade
wind. In the rear the forest is a wall of darkness dividing
the world. Only when the eye becomes accustomed to
the gloom can the outlines of separate trunks of the nearest trees be made out, enormous pillars of deeper blackness. A somber monotone of wind lost in the leaves
moans in the air. Yet this sound serves but to intensify*

*the impression of the forest's relentless immobility, to
form a background throwing into relief its brooding, implacable silence.*

JONES *enters from the left, walking rapidly. He stops as he
nears the edge of the forest, looks around him quickly,
peering into the dark as if searching for some familiar
landmark. Then, apparently satisfied that he is where he
ought to be, he throws himself on the ground, dog-tired.*

Well, heah I is. In de nick o' time, too! Little mo' an' it'd
be blacker'n de ace of spades heahabouts. [*He pulls a
bandana handkerchief from his hip pocket and mops
off his perspiring face.*] Sho! Gimme air! I'se tuck-
ered out sho' 'nuf. Dat soft Emperor job ain't no   5
trainin' fo' a long hike ovah dat plain in de brilin'
sun. [*Then with a chuckle*] Cheer up, nigger, der
worst is yet to come. [*He lifts his head and stares
at the forest. His chuckle peters out abruptly. In a
tone of awe*] My goodness, look at dem woods, will   10
you? Dat no-count Smithers said dey'd be black an'
he sho' called de turn. [*Turning away from them
quickly, and looking down at his feet, he snatches at
a chance to change the subject—solicitously*] Feet,
yo' is holdin' up yo' end fine an' I sutinly hopes you   15
ain't blisterin' none. It's time you git a rest. [*He
takes off his shoes, his eyes studiously avoiding the
forest. He feels of the soles of his feet gingerly.*] You
is still in de pink—only a little mite feverish. Cool

you' self. Remember yo' done got a long journey yit 20
befo' yo'. [*He sits in a weary attitude, listening to
the rhythmic beating of the tom-tom. He grumbles
in a loud tone to cover up a growing uneasiness.*]
Bush niggers! Wonder dey wouldn't git sick o'
beatin' dat drum. Sound louder, seem like. I won- 25
der if dey's startin' after me? [*He scrambles to
his feet, looking back across the plain.*] Couldn't see
dem now, nohow, if dey was hundred feet away.
[*Then shaking himself like a wet dog to get rid of
these depressing thoughts.*] Sho', dey's miles an' miles 30
behind. What yo' gittin' fidgetty about? [*But he
sits down and begins to lace up his shoes in great haste,
all the time muttering reassuringly.*] You know
what? Yo' belly is empty, dat's what's de matter wid
you. Come time to eat! Wid nothin' but wind on 35
yo' stumach, o' course yo' feels jiggedy. Well, we
eats right heah an' now soon's I gits dese pesky shoes
laced up. [*He finishes lacing up his shoes.*] Dere!
Now le's see! [*Gets on his hands and knees and
searches the ground around him with his eyes.*] 40
White stone, white stone, where is yo'? [*He sees the
first white stone and crawls to it—with satisfaction.*]
Heah yo' is! I knowed dis was de right place. Box
of grub, come to me. [*He turns over the stone and
feels in under it—in a tone of dismay*] Ain't heah! 45
Gorry, is I in de right place or isn't I? Dere's 'nother
stone. Guess dat's it. [*He scrambles to the next stone

and turns it over.] Ain't heah, neither! Grub, whar is yo'? Ain't heah. Gorry, has I got to go hungry into dem woods—all de night? [*While he is talking he* 50 *scrambles from one stone to another, turning them over in frantic haste. Finally he jumps to his feet excitedly.*] Is I lost de place? Must have! But how dat happen when I was followin' de trail across de plain in broad daylight? [*Almost plaintively*] I'se 55 hungry, I is! I gotta git my feed. Whar's my strength gonna come from if I doesn't? Gorry, I gotta find dat grub high an' low somehow! Why it come dark so quick like dat? Can't see nothin'. [*He scratches a match on his trousers and peers about* 60 *him. The rate of the beat of the far-off tom-tom increases perceptibly as he does so. He mutters in a bewildered voice.*] How come all dese white stones come heah when I only remembers one? [*Suddenly, with a frightened gasp, he flings the match on the* 65 *ground and stamps on it.*] Nigger, is yo' gone crazy mad? Is you lightin' matches to show dem whar you is? Fo' Lawd's sake, use yo' haid. Gorry, I'se got to be careful! [*He stares at the plain behind him apprehensively, his hand on his revolver.*] But how 70 come all dese white stones? And whar's dat tin box o' grub I hid all wrapped up in oilcloth?

While his back is turned, the LITTLE FORMLESS FEARS *creep out from the deeper blackness of the forest. They are black, shapeless; only their glittering little eyes can be seen. If they have any describable form at all it is that of a grub-worm about the size of a creeping child. They move noiselessly, but with deliberate, painful effort, striving to raise themselves on end, failing and sinking prone again.* Jones *turns about to face the forest. He stares up at the tops of the trees, seeking vainly to discover his whereabouts by their conformation.*

Can't tell nothin' from dem trees! Gorry, nothin' 'round heah look like I evah seed it befo'. I'se done lost de place sho' nuff! [*With mournful foreboding*] It's   75 mighty queer! It's mighty queer! [*With sudden forced defiance—in an angry tone*] Woods, is yo' tryin' to put somethin' ovah on me?

From the formless creatures on the ground in front of him comes a tiny gale of low mocking laughter like a rustling of leaves. They squirm upward toward him in twisted attitudes. Jones *looks down, leaps backward with a yell of terror, yanking out his revolver as he does so—in a quavering voice.*

What's dat? Who's dar? What's you? Git away from me befo' I shoots yo' up! Yo' don't?—   80

He fires. There is a flash, a loud report, then silence, broken only by the far-off quickened throb of the tom-tom. The formless creatures have scurried back into the forest. Jones *remains fixed in his position, listening intently.*

The sound of the shot, the reassuring feel of the revolver
in his hand have somewhat restored his shaken nerve.
He addresses himself with renewed confidence:

Dey're gone. Dat shot fix 'em. Dey was only little animals—little wild pigs, I reckon. Dey've maybe rooted
out yo' grub an' eat it. Sho', yo' fool nigger, what yo'
think dey is—ha'nts? [*Excitedly*] Gorry, you give de
game away when yo' fire dat shot. Dem niggers heah   85
dat fo' su'tin! Time yo' beat it in de woods widout
no long waits. [*He starts for the forest—hesitates*
before the plunge—then urging himself in with man-
ful resolution.] Git in, nigger! What yo' skeered at?
Ain't nothin' dere but de trees! Git in! [*He plunges*   90
boldly into the forest.]

SCENE THREE

Nine o'clock. In the forest. The moon has just risen. Its
beams drifting through the canopy of leaves make a
barely perceptible, suffused eerie glow. A dense low wall
of underbrush and creepers is in the nearer foreground
fencing in a small triangular clearing. Beyond this is the
massed blackness of the forest like an encompassing bar-
rier. A path is dimly discerned leading down to the
clearing from left, rear, and winding away from it again

*toward the right. As the scene opens nothing can be
distinctly made out. Except for the beating of the tom-
tom, which is a trifle louder and quicker than in the
previous scene, there is silence, broken every few seconds
by a queer, clicking sound. Then gradually the figure of
the negro* JEFF *can be discerned crouching on his haunches
at the rear of the triangle. He is middle-aged, thin,
brown in color, is dressed in a Pullman porter's uniform,
cap, etc. He is throwing a pair of dice on the ground
before him, picking them up, shaking them, casting them
out with the regular, rigid, mechanical movements of an
automaton. The heavy, plodding footsteps of some one
approaching along the trail from the left are heard, and*
JONES' *voice, pitched in a slightly higher key and strained
in a cheering effort to overcome its own tremors.*

De moon's rizen. Does yo' heah dat, nigger? Yo' gits
more light from dis out. No mo' buttin' yo' fool head
agin' de trunks an' scratchin' de hide off yo' legs in de
bushes. Now yo' sees whar yo'se gwine. So cheer
up! From now on yo' has a snap. [*He steps just   5
to the rear of the triangular clearing and mops off his
face on his sleeve. He has lost his Panama hat. His
face is scratched, his brilliant uniform shows several
large rents.*] What time's it gittin' to be, I wonder?
I dassent light no match to find out. Phoo'. It's   10
wa'm, an' dat's a fac'! [*Wearily*] How long I been
makin' tracks in dese woods? Must be hours an'

hours. Seems like fo'evah! Yit can't be, when de moon's jes' riz. Dis am a long night fo' yo', yo' Majesty! [*With a mournful chuckle*] Majesty! Der 15 ain't much majesty 'bout dis baby now. [*With attempted cheerfulness*] Never min'. It's all part o' de game. Dis night come to an end like everythin' else. An' when yo' gits dar safe an' has dat bank-roll in yo' hands, yo' laughs at all dis. [*He starts* 20 *to whistle, but checks himself abruptly.*] What yo' whistlin' for, yo' po' dope? Want all de worl' to heah yo'? [*He stops talking to listen.*] Heah dat ole drum! Sho' gits nearer from de sound. Dey're packin' it along wid 'em. Time fo' me to move. 25 [*He takes a step forward, then stops—worriedly.*] What's dat odder queer clicketty sound I heah? Der it is! Sound close! Sound like—fo' God sake, sound like some nigger was shakin' crap! [*Frightenedly*] I better beat it quick when I gits dem notions. [*He* 30 *walks quickly into the clear space—then stands transfixed as he sees* JEFF—*in a terrified gasp.*] Who dar? Who dat? Is dat yo', Jeff? [*Starting toward the other, forgetful for a moment of his surroundings and really believing it is a living man that he sees—* 35 *in a tone of happy relief.*] Jeff! I'se sho' mighty glad to see yo'! Dey tol' me yo' done died from dat razor cut I gives you. [*Stopping suddenly, bewilderedly*] But how come you to be heah, nigger? [*He stares* **fascinatedly** *at the other, who continues his mechani-* 40

cal play with the dice. Jones' *eyes begin to roll wildly.*
He stutters] Ain't you gwine—look up—can't you
speak to me? Is you—is you—a ha'nt? [*He jerks
out his revolver in a frenzy of terrified rage.*] Nigger, I kills yo' dead once. Has I got to kill yo'   45
agin? You take it, den. [*He fires. When the
smoke clears away* Jeff *has disappeared.* Jones
stands trembling—then with a certain reassurance]
He's gone, anyway. Ha'nt or no ha'nt, dat shot fix
him. [*The beat of the far-off tom-tom is perceptibly*   50
louder and more rapid. Jones *becomes conscious of*
it—with a start, looking back over his shoulder.]
Dey's gittin' near! Dey're comin' fast! An' heah I is
shootin' shots to let 'em know jes' whar I is. Oh,
Gorry, I'se got to run. [*Forgetting the path, he*   55
plunges wildly into the underbrush in the rear and
disappears in the shadow.]

THE EMPEROR JONES
FROM THE YALE UNIVERSITY PRODUCTION

THE CHAIN GANG SCENE
FROM THE YALE UNIVERSITY PRODUCTION

SCENE FOUR

*Eleven o'clock. In the forest. A wide dirt road runs diag-
onally from right, front, to left, rear. Rising sheer on
both sides the forest walls it in. The moon is now up.
Under its light the road glimmers ghastly and unreal.
It is as if the forest had stood aside momentarily to let
the road pass through and accomplish its veiled purpose.
This done, the forest will fold in upon itself again and
the road will be no more.* JONES *stumbles in from the
forest on the right. His uniform is ragged and torn. He
looks about him with numbed surprise when he sees the
road, his eyes blinking in the bright moonlight. He flops
down exhaustedly and pants heavily for a while. Then
with sudden anger:*

I'm meltin' wid heat! Runnin' an' runnin' an' runnin'!
Damn dis heah coat! Like a straitjacket! [*He tears
off his coat and flings it away from him, revealing
himself stripped to the waist.*] Dere! Dat's better!
Now I kin breathe! [*Looking down at his feet, the*   5
spurs catch his eye.] An' to hell wid dese high-
fangled spurs. Dey're what's been a-trippin' me up
an' breakin' my neck. [*He unstraps and flings them
away disgustedly.*] Dere! I gits rid o' dem frippety
Emperor trappin's an' I travels lighter. Lawd! I'se   10
tired! [*After a pause, listening to the insistent beat
of the tom-tom in the distance.*] I must 'a put some

distance between myself an' dem—runnin' like dat—
an' yet—dat damn drum sound jes' de same—nearer,
even. Well, I guess I a'most holds my lead, anyhow. 15
Dey won't never kotch up. [*With a sigh*] If on'y
my fool legs stands up. Oh, I'se sorry I evah went in
for dis. Dat Emperor job is sho' hard to shake. [*He
looks around him suspiciously.*] How'd dis road
evah git heah? Good, level road, too. I never re- 20
members seein' it befo'. [*Shaking his head apprehensively.*] Dese woods is sho' full o' de queerest
things at night. [*With sudden terror*] Lawd God,
don't let me see no more o' dem ha'nts. Dey gits
my goat! [*Then trying to talk himself into confi-* 25
dence.] Ha'nts! Yo' fool nigger, dey ain't no such
things! Don't de Baptist parson tell you dat many
time? Is yo' civilized, or is yo' like dese ign'rent black
niggers heah? Sho'! Dat was all in yo' own head.
Wasn't nothin' there! Wasn't no Jeff! Know what? 30
Yo' jus' get seein' dem thing 'cause yo' belly's empty
an' you's sick wid hunger inside. Hunger 'fects yo'
head an' yo' eyes. Any fool know dat. [*Then
pleading fervently*] But bless God, I don't come across
no more o' dem, whatever dey is! [*Then cautiously*] 35
Rest! Don't talk! Rest! You needs it. Den yo' gits
on yo' way again. [*Looking at the moon*] Night's
half gone a'most. Yo' hits de coast in de mawning!
Den you'se all safe.

*From the right forward a small gang of negroes enter. They
are dressed in striped convict suits, their heads are shaven,
one leg drags limpingly, shackled to a heavy ball and
chain. Some carry picks, the others shovels. They are
followed by a white man dressed in the uniform of a
prison guard. A Winchester rifle is slung across his
shoulders and he carries a heavy whip. At a signal from
the guard they stop on the road opposite to where JONES
is sitting. JONES, who has been staring up at the sky,
unmindful of their noiseless approach, suddenly looks
down and sees them. His eyes pop out, he tries to get
to his feet and fly, but sinks back, too numbed by fright
to move. His voice catches in a choking prayer.*

Lawd Jesus!   40

*The prison guard cracks his whip—noiselessly—and at that
signal all the convicts start to work on the road. They
swing their picks, they shovel, but not a sound comes
from their labor. Their movements, like those of JEFF
in the preceding scene, are those of automatons—rigid,
slow, and mechanical. The prison guard points sternly
at JONES with his whip, motions him to take his place
among the other shovelers. JONES gets to his feet in a
hypnotized stupor. He mumbles subserviently:*

Yes, suh! Yes, suh! I'se comin'!

*As he shuffles, dragging one foot, over to his place, he curses
under his breath with rage and hatred.*

God damn yo' soul, I gits even wid yo' yit, sometime.

As if there was a shovel in his hand, he goes through weary, mechanical gestures of digging up dirt and throwing it to the roadside. Suddenly the guard approaches him angrily, threateningly. He raises his whip and lashes Jones *viciously across the shoulders with it.* Jones *winces with pain and cowers abjectly. The guard turns his back on him and walks away contemptuously. Instantly* Jones *straightens up. With arms upraised, as if his shovel were a club in his hands, he springs murderously at the unsuspecting guard. In the act of crashing down his shovel on the white man's skull,* Jones *suddenly becomes aware that his hands are empty. He cries despairingly:*

Whar's my shovel? Gimme my shovel 'till I splits his damn head! [*Appealing to his fellow convicts*] Gimme a shovel, one o' yo' fo' God's sake! 45

They stand fixed in motionless attitudes, their eyes on the ground. The guard seems to wait expectantly, his back turned to the attacker. Jones *bellows his baffled terrified rage, tugging frantically at his revolver.*

I kills you, you white debil, if it's de last thing I evah does! Ghost or debil, I kill you agin!

He frees the revolver and fires pointblank at the guard's back. Instantly the walls of the forest close in from both sides, the road and the figures of the convict gang are blotted out in an enshrouding darkness. The only sounds are a

crashing in the underbrush as Jones *leaps away in mad
flight and the throbbing of the tom-tom, still far distant,
but increased in volume of sound and rapidity of beat.*

SCENE FIVE

*One o'clock. A large circular clearing, enclosed by the serried
ranks of lofty, gigantic trunks of tall trees whose tops are
lost to view. In the center is a big dead stump, worn by
time into a curious resemblance to an auction block. The
moon floods the clearing with a clear light.* Jones *forces
his way in through the forest on the left. He looks wildly
about the clearing with hunted, fearful glances. His pants
are in tatters, his shoes cut and misshapen, flapping about
his feet. He slinks cautiously to the stump in the center
and sits down in a tense position, ready for instant flight.
Then he holds his head in his hands and rocks back and
forth, moaning to himself miserably.*

Oh, Lawd, Lawd! Oh Lawd, Lawd! [*Suddenly he
throws himself on his knees and raises his clasped
hands to the sky—in a voice of agonized pleading.*]
Lawd, Jesus, heah my prayer! I'se a poor sinner, a
poor sinner! I knows I done wrong, I knows it!   5
When I cotches Jeff cheatin' wid loaded dice my
anger overcomes me an' I kills him dead! Lawd, I
done wrong! When dat guard hits me wid de whip,

my anger overcomes me, and I kills him dead. Lawd,
I done wrong! An' down heah whar dese fool bush   10
niggers raises me up to the seat o' de mighty, I steals
all I could grab. Lawd, I done wrong! I knows it!
I'se sorry! Forgive me, Lawd! Forgive dis po' sinner! [*Then beseeching terrifiedly*] An' keep dem
away, Lawd! Keep dem away from me! An' stop   15
dat drum soundin' in my ears! Dat begin to sound
ha'nted, too. [*He gets to his feet, evidently slightly
reassured by his prayer—with attempted confidence*]
De Lawd'll preserve me from dem ha'nts after dis.
[*Sits down on the stump again.*] I ain't skeered o'   20
real men. Let dem come. But dem odders— [*He
shudders—then looks down at his feet, working his
toes inside the shoes—with a groan*] Oh, my po'
feet! Dem shoes ain't no use no more 'ceptin' to hurt.
I'se better off widout dem. [*He unlaces them and   25
pulls them off—holds the wrecks of the shoes in his
hand and regards them mournfully.*] You was real
A-one patin' leather, too. Look at yo' now. Emperor,
you'se gittin' mighty low!

*He sighs dejectedly and remains with bowed shoulders, star-
   ing down at the shoes in his hands as if reluctant to
   throw them away. While his attention is thus occupied,
   a crowd of figures silently enter the clearing from all sides.
   All are dressed in Southern costumes of the period of the
   fifties of the last century. There are middle-aged men*

who are evidently well-to-do planters. There is one
spruce, authoritative individual—the AUCTIONEER. There
is a crowd of curious spectators, chiefly young belles and
dandies who have come to the slave market for diversion.
All exchange courtly greetings in dumb show and chat
silently together. There is something stiff, rigid, unreal,
marionettish about their movements. They group themselves about the stump. Finally a batch of slaves are led
in from the left by an attendant—three men of different
ages, two women, one with a baby in her arms, nursing.
They are placed to the left of the stump, beside JONES.

The WHITE PLANTERS look them over appraisingly as if they
were cattle, and exchange judgments on each. The dandies point with their fingers and make witty remarks.
The belles titter bewitchingly. All this in silence save for
the ominous throb of the tom-tom. The AUCTIONEER holds
up his hand, taking his place at the stump. The groups
strain forward attentively. He touches JONES on the
shoulder peremptorily, motioning for him to stand on
the stump—the auction block. JONES looks up, sees the
figures on all sides, looks wildly for some opening to
escape, sees none, screams and leaps madly to the top of the
stump to get as far away from them as possible. He stands
there, cowering, paralyzed with horror. The AUCTIONEER
begins his silent spiel. He points to JONES, appeals to the
PLANTERS to see for themselves. Here is a good field hand,
sound in wind and limb, as they can see. Very strong

*still, in spite of his being middle-aged. Look at that back.
Look at those shoulders. Look at the muscles in his arms
and his sturdy legs. Capable of any amount of hard
labor. Moreover, of a good disposition, intelligent and
tractable. Will any gentleman start the bidding? The*
Planters *raise their fingers, make their bids. They are
apparently all eager to possess* Jones. *The bidding is
lively, the crowd interested. While this has been going
on,* Jones *has been seized by the courage of desperation.
He dares to look down and around him. Over his face
abject terror gives way to mystification, to gradual realization—stutteringly:*

What yo' all doin', white folks? What's all dis? What   30
yo' all lookin' at me fo'? What yo' doin' wid me,
anyhow? [*Suddenly convulsed with raging hatred
and fear*] Is dis a auction? Is yo' sellin' me like dey
uster befo' de war? [*Jerking out his revolver just as
the* Auctioneer *knocks him down to one of the*   35
planters—glaring from him to the purchasers] An'
you sells me? An' *you* buys me? I shows you I'se a
free nigger, damn yo' souls! [*He fires at the* Auctioneer *and at the* Planter *with such rapidity that the
two shots are almost simultaneous. As if this were*   40
*a signal, the walls of the forest fold in. Only black-
ness remains and silence broken by* Jones *as he rushes
off, crying with fear—and by the quickened, ever
louder beat of the tom-tom.*]

SCENE SIX

Three o'clock. A cleared space in the forest. The limbs of the trees meet over it, forming a low ceiling about five feet from the ground. The interlocked ropes of creepers reaching upward to entwine the tree trunks give an arched appearance to the sides. The space this encloses is like the dark, noisome hold of some ancient vessel. The moonlight is almost completely shut out and only a vague, wan light filters through. There is the noise of some one approaching from the left, stumbling and crawling through the undergrowth. Jones' voice is heard between chattering moans.

Oh, Lawd, what I gwine do now? Ain't got no bullet left on'y de silver one. If mo' o' dem ha'nts come after me, how I gwine skeer dem away? Oh, Lawd, on'y de silver one left—an' I gotta save dat fo' luck. If I shoots dat one I'm a goner sho'! Lawd, it's black   5 heah! Whar's de moon? Oh, Lawd, don't dis night evah come to an end? [*By the sounds he is feeling his way cautiously forward.*] Dere! Dis feels like a clear space. I gotta lie down an' rest. I don't care if dem niggers does catch me. I gotta rest.   10

He is well forward now where his figure can be dimly made out. His pants have been so torn away that what is left of them is no better than a breech cloth. He flings himself full length, face downward on the ground, panting with exhaustion. *Gradually it seems to grow lighter in the enclosed space, and two rows of seated figures can be seen behind* JONES. *They are sitting in crumpled, despairing attitudes, hunched facing one another, with their backs touching the forest walls as if they were shackled to them. All are negroes, naked save for loin cloths. At first they are silent and motionless. Then they begin to sway slowly forward toward each other and back again in unison, as if they were laxly letting themselves follow the long roll of a ship at sea. At the same time, a low, melancholy murmur rises among them, increasing gradually by rhythmic degrees, which seem to be directed and controlled by the throb of the tom-tom in the distance, to a long, tremendous wail of despair that reaches a certain pitch, unbearably acute, then falls by slow gradations of tone into silence and is taken up again.* JONES *starts, looks up, sees the figures, and throws himself down again to shut out the sight. A shudder of terror shakes his whole body as the wail rises up about him again. But the next time, his voice, as if under some uncanny compulsion, starts with the others. As their chorus lifts he rises to a sitting posture similar to the others, swaying back and forth. His voice reaches the highest pitch of sorrow, of desolation. The light fades out, the other voices cease, and only darkness is left.* JONES *can be heard scrambling to his feet and running off, his voice sinking down the scale and receding as he moves farther and farther away in the forest. The tom-tom beats louder, quicker, with a more insistent, triumphant pulsation.*

SCENE SIX
FROM THE SCREEN PRODUCTION

THE JUNGLE
FROM THE UNIVERSITY OF NEBRASKA PRODUCTION

SCENE SEVEN

*Five o'clock. The foot of a gigantic tree by the edge of a
great river. A rough structure of boulders like an altar is
by the tree. The raised river bank is in the nearer background. Beyond this the surface of the river spreads out
brilliant and unruffled in the moonlight, blotted out and
merged into a veil of bluish mist in the distance.* JONES'
*voice is heard from the left, rising and falling in the
long, despairing wail of the chained slaves, to the rhythmic beat of the tom-tom. As his voice sinks into silence
he enters the open space. The expression of his face is
fixed and stony, his eyes have an obsessed glare, he moves
with a strange deliberation like a sleep-walker or one in
a trance. He looks around at the tree, the rough stone
altar, the moonlit surface of the river beyond, and passes
his hand over his head with a vague gesture of puzzled
bewilderment. Then, as if in obedience to some obscure
impulse, he sinks into a kneeling, devotional posture before the altar. Then he seems to come to himself partly,
to have an uncertain realization of what he is doing, for
he straightens up and stares about him horrifiedly—in an
incoherent mumble.*

What—what is I doin'? What is—dis place? Seems like
—seems like I know dat tree—an' dem stones—an' de
river. I remember—seems like I been heah befo'.

[*Tremblingly*] Oh, Gorry, I'se skeered in dis place!   5
I'se skeered! Oh, Lawd, pertect dis sinner!

*Crawling away from the altar, he cowers close to the ground,
his face hidden, his shoulders heaving with sobs of hys-
terical fright. From behind the trunk of the tree, as if he
had sprung out of it, the figure of the* CONGO WITCH-
DOCTOR *appears. He is wizened and old, naked except
for the fur of some small animal tied about his waist, its
bushy tail hanging down in front. His body is stained
all over a bright red. Antelope horns are on each side of
his head, branching upward. In one hand he carries a
bone rattle, in the other a charm stick with a bunch of
white cockatoo feathers tied to the end. A great number of glass beads and bone ornaments are about his neck,
ears, wrists, and ankles. He struts noiselessly with a queer
prancing step to a position in the clear ground between*
JONES *and altar. Then with a preliminary, summoning
stamp of his foot on the earth, he begins to dance and to
chant. As if in response to his summons the beating of
the tom-tom grows to a fierce, exultant boom whose
throbs seem to fill the air with vibrating rhythm.* JONES
*looks up, starts to spring to his feet, reaches a half-
kneeling, half-squatting position, and remains rigidly
fixed there, paralyzed with awed fascination by this new
apparition. The* WITCH-DOCTOR *sways, stamping with his
foot, his bone rattle clicking the time. His voice rises and
falls in a weird, monotonous croon, without articulate word*

division. Gradually his dance becomes clearly one of a narrative in pantomime, his croon is an incantation, a charm to allay the fierceness of some implacable deity demanding sacrifice. He flees, he is pursued by devils, he hides, he flees again. Ever wilder and wilder becomes his flight, nearer and nearer draws the pursuing evil, more and more the spirit of terror gains possession of him. His croon, rising to intensity, is punctuated by shrill cries. JONES *has become completely hypnotized. His voice joins in the incantation, in the cries; he beats time with his hands and sways his body to and fro from the waist. The whole spirit and meaning of the dance has entered into him, has become his spirit. Finally the theme of the pantomime halts, on a howl of despair, and is taken up again in a note of savage hope. There is a salvation. The forces of evil demand sacrifice. They must be appeased. The* WITCH-DOCTOR *points with his wand to the sacred tree, to the river beyond, to the altar, and finally to* JONES *with a ferocious command.* JONES *seems to sense the meaning of this. It is he who must offer himself for sacrifice. He beats his forehead abjectly to the ground, moaning hysterically.*

Mercy, Oh Lawd! Mercy! Mercy on dis po' sinner!

The WITCH-DOCTOR *springs to the river banks. He stretches out his arms and calls to some god within its depths. Then he starts backward slowly, his arms remaining out. A huge head of a crocodile appears over the bank and its eyes, glittering greenly, fasten upon* Jones. *He stares into them fascinatedly. The* Witch-Doctor *prances up to him, touches him with his wand, motions with hideous command toward the waiting monster.* Jones *squirms on his belly nearer and nearer, moaning continually:*

Mercy, Lawd! Mercy!

The crocodile heaves more of his enormous hulk onto the land. Jones *squirms toward him. The* Witch-Doctor's *voice shrills out in furious exultation, the tom-tom beats madly.* Jones *cries out in fierce, exhausted spasms of anguished pleading:*

Lawd, save me! Lawd Jesus, heah my prayer!

Immediately, in answer to his prayer, comes the thought of the one bullet left him. He snatches at his hip, shouting defiantly:

De silver bullet! Yo' don't git me yit!   10

He fires at the green eyes in front of him. The head of the crocodile sinks back behind the river bank, the Witch-Doctor *springs behind the sacred tree and disappears.* Jones *lies with his face to the ground, his arms outstretched, whimpering with fear as the throb of the tom-tom fills the silence about him with a somber pulsation, a baffled but revengeful power.*

THE WITCH-DOCTOR
FROM THE YALE UNIVERSITY PRODUCTION

It has been proven conclusively that man cannot fly!

SCENE EIGHT

*Dawn. Same as Scene Two, the dividing line of forest and
plain. The nearest tree trunks are dimly revealed, but
the forest behind them is still a mass of glooming shadow.
The tom-tom seems on the very spot, so loud and con-
tinuously vibrating are its beats. LEM enters from the
left, followed by a small squad of his soldiers, and by the
Cockney trader, SMITHERS. LEM is a heavy-set, ape-faced
old savage of the extreme African type, dressed only in a
loin cloth. A revolver and cartridge belt are about his
waist. His soldiers are in different degrees of rag-
concealed nakedness. All wear broad palm leaf hats.
Each one carries a rifle. SMITHERS is the same as in Scene
One. One of the soldiers, evidently a tracker, is peering
about keenly on the ground. He grunts and points to the
spot where JONES entered the forest. LEM and SMITHERS
come to look.*

Smithers. [*After a glance, turns away in disgust.*] That's
     where 'e went in right enough. Much good it'll do
     yer. 'E's miles orf by this an' safe to the coast, damn
     'is 'ide. I tole yer ye'd lose 'im, didn't I?—wastin' the
     'ole bloomin' night beatin' yer bloody drum and   5
     castin' yer silly spells! Gawd blimey, wot a pack!
Lem. [*Gutturally*] We kotch him. You see. [*He makes*

*a motion to his soldiers, who squat down on their
haunches in a semi-circle.*]

Smithers. [*Exasperatedly*] Well, ain't yer goin' in an'   10
'unt 'im in the woods? What the 'ell's the good of
waitin'?

Lem. [*Imperturbably—squatting down himself*] We
kotch him.

Smithers. [*Turning away from him contemptuously*]   15
Aw! Garn! 'E's a better man than the lot o' you put
together. I 'ates the sight o' 'im, but I'll say that for
'im.

*A sound of snapping twigs comes from the forest. The sol-
diers jump to their feet, cocking their rifles alertly.* LEM
*remains sitting with an imperturbable expression, but
listening intently. The sound from the woods is re-
peated.* LEM *makes a quick signal with his hand. His
followers creep quickly but noiselessly into the forest,
scattering so that each enters at a different spot.*

Smithers. [*In the silence that follows—in a contemptuous
whisper*] You ain't thinkin' that would be 'im, I 'ope?   20
Lem. [*Calmly*] We kotch him.
Smithers. Blarsted fat 'eads! [*Then after a second's
thought—wonderingly*] Still an' all, it might happen.
If 'e lost 'is bloody way in these stinkin' woods 'e'd
likely turn in a circle without 'is knowin' it. They all   25
does.
Lem. [*Peremptorily*] S-s-s-h-h!

*The report of several rifles sounds from the forest, followed a
    second later by savage, exultant yells. The beating of
    the tom-tom abruptly ceases.* Lem *looks up at the white
    man with a grin of satisfaction.*

We kotch him.   Him dead.

Smithers. [*With a snarl*] 'Ow d'yer know it's 'im an' 'ow
    d'yer know 'e's dead?   30

Lem. My men's dey got 'um silver bullets.   Dey kill him
    shore.

Smithers. [*Astonished*] They got silver bullets?

Lem. Lead bullets no kill him.   He got um strong charm.
    I took um money, make um silver bullet, make um   35
    strong charm, too.

Smithers. [*Light breaking upon him*] So that's wot you
    was up to all night, wot?   You was scared to put after
    'im till you'd molded silver bullets, eh?

Lem. [*Simply stating a fact*] Yes. Him got strong charm.   40
    Lead no good.

Smithers. [*Slapping his thigh and guffawing*] Haw-haw!
    If yer don't beat al 'ell!   [*Then recovering himself—
    scornfully*] I'll bet you it ain't 'im they shot at all,
    yer bleedin' looney!   45

Lem. [*Calmly*] Dey come bring him now.

The soldiers come out of the forest, carrying Jones' *limp body.
    There is a little reddish-purple hole under his left breast.
    He is dead.   They carry him to* Lem, *who examines his*

body with great satisfaction. SMITHERS *leans over his shoulder—in a tone of frightened awe:*

Well, they did for yer right enough, Jonesy, me lad! Dead as a 'erring! [*Mockingly*] Where's yer 'igh an' mighty airs now, yer bloomin' Majesty? [*Then with a grin*] Silver bullets! Gawd blimey, but yer 50 died in the 'eight o' style, any 'ow!

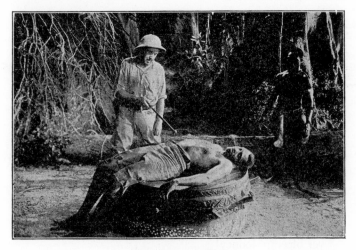

THE FINAL SCENE
FROM THE SCREEN PRODUCTION

QUESTIONS FOR COMPARATIVE STUDY

Macbeth—The Emperor Jones

Destiny

Among the ancient Greeks, destiny was believed to be the force that ruled a man's life. Often his destiny was made known to him by prophecies. When this was the case there were three courses of action open to him: he could do nothing and let things take their course; he could exert his will in helping to achieve his destiny; he could strive to oppose it. Macbeth's destiny was to become King, to be safe from all born of woman, to suffer Banquo's descendants to reign after him. Jones's destiny was to become Emperor for the purpose of enriching himself, to be forced to flee to save his gains, to be invulnerable, according to his own boast, except by a silver bullet.

1. What actions of Macbeth and Jones were in accordance with the first course of action?
2. What according to the second?
3. What according to the third?
4. In what ways were their punishments similar?
5. Discuss the justice of the punishment in each case.

Ambition

6. At what stage in the plays had each attained his chief ambition? Why is this so much earlier in the play in the case of Jones?
7. What had each done to achieve his ambition?
8. What proportion of each play is occupied with the hero's efforts to conserve the gains already made?
9. Why is this proportion so much greater in the case of Jones?

The Apparitions

10. The apparitions in *Macbeth,* Act IV, Scene 1, are all in the nature of prophecies of what is to come; those in *The Emperor Jones* are reenactments of events in the past. Discuss the significance of this difference.

11. Why do the apparitions in *Macbeth* talk, while those in the other play do not?

12. Point out the similarities and differences in the scenes where the ghost of Banquo and the ghost of Jeff appear.

13. Compare the Elizabethan witch lore as exemplified in the Weird Sisters with the African witch lore as exemplified in the Witch-Doctor.

General Questions

14. Compare the use of soliloquy in the two plays.

15. Compare the rapid degradation and degeneration of Macbeth and Jones.

16. Find a line in *Macbeth* parallel to this from Scene 4 of *The Emperor Jones:* "Lawd God, don't let me see no more of dem ha'nts!"

17. Find a line in *Macbeth* parallel to this from Scene 5 of *The Emperor Jones:* "I ain't skeered o' real men. Let dem come. But dem odders—."

18. Macbeth places full reliance for his safety upon the prophecy of the Weird Sisters. Does Jones have any confidence in the "silver bullet"?

19. What preparations has Jones made for escape? Did Macbeth make any?

20. Did both Macbeth and Jones have confidence in themselves?

21. What is the first thing to shake Jones's confidence? Macbeth's?

22. Discuss the element of superstition in each play.

23. What mistakes did Macbeth make in attaining his position? Compare with those of Jones.

24. Does Macbeth wish to die before the end of the play? Does Jones?

25. When does misfortune begin to overtake Macbeth? Jones?

26. Discuss the two plays as tragedies of the triumph of right.

27. Is there any comic relief provided in *The Emperor Jones?* In *Macbeth?*

28. Do you care more about the death of Macbeth or of Jones? Why?

29. Is death inevitable in each case? Explain.

30. Is retribution an important element in each play? Explain.

31. Compare the two plays as to spectacular effects, dramatic qualities, truthful representation of life, and characterization.

32. Compare Macbeth and Jones as to their estimate of their adversaries.

33. What motives impell Macbeth? Jones?

34. Act III, Scene 1 is the only place where Shakespeare shows us the King and Queen in their royal robes. Compare with Jones in Scene 1. Do they "sit easily"?

35. Is remorse the real base of all Macbeth's feeling, or simply fear? Which is the case in Jones?

36. Does Jones ever have any regrets? Does Macbeth?

37. When and where does Macbeth assume a forced gayety? Jones?

COMPOSITION TOPICS

1. The character of Macbeth and of the Emperor Jones. A comparison.

2. The element of fear in the two plays.

3. Superstition in *Macbeth* and in *The Emperor Jones.*

4. The appeal of the two plays.

5. Jones and Macbeth as victims of Destiny.
6. External Nature a powerful factor in obtaining dramatic effect.
7. Dramatic moments in the two plays.
8. Character contrasts in the two plays.
9. Fulfillment of the prophecies.
10. Notable modern presentations.
11. Ambition in Macbeth and in Emperor Jones.

Prove or disprove the following

12. These plays are "a grand escape from realism."
13. These plays are alike in more ways than they are different.
14. Both plays present "royal and human tragedy."
15. A successful ruler must be ruthless.

COMMENTS AND QUESTIONS

Macbeth

Act I—Scene 1

The first scene gives the atmosphere of the play to follow. The desolate place, the storm, the evil beings who appear, all prepare us for a dark and tragic story. Note, too, that there is specific preparation for a later scene, the meeting with Macbeth. And we learn that a battle is being fought elsewhere, but that it will be ended before sunset. All this is given to us in ten lines. It shows how compressed a play is as compared to a novel.

What is the meaning of the line,

"Fair is foul, and foul is fair."

Scene 2

What new characters appear in this scene?

Here we learn more about the battle: the forces of the king are fighting against troops under Macdonwald, a Scottish rebel, and also against an invading army from Norway. Although Macbeth does not appear in this scene, we learn something about him: what is it? How does the close of the scene prepare us for something to come?

Scene 3

This scene may be divided into two parts, the first part ending at the entrance of Macbeth. From this part, what knowledge do we gain about the witches? It was commonly believed in

Shakespeare's time that witches had power to bring sickness or even death upon animals or persons.

The second part of the scene opens with the entrance of Macbeth and Banquo. Note that Banquo is the first to speak to the witches, but they place their fingers on their lips; when Macbeth addresses them they reply. What does this suggest?

Observe that Macbeth starts at the predictions of the witches: had they read his secret thoughts?

After the witches disappear, Ross enters and announces that Macbeth is to be Thane of Cawdor. What effect would this have upon Macbeth?

Note carefully Macbeth's words spoken aside: such speeches are the means a dramatist uses to let us read a person's thoughts. If Macbeth wished to attain the throne, two courses were open to him: to exert himself to attain it, or to let things drift, thinking that, just as he became Thane of Cawdor without effort on his part, so he might become king. He was of royal descent, and had won renown in battle: if anything happened to Duncan, Macbeth would have a strong claim to consideration. Which of the two courses named above has Macbeth decided to follow?

Scene 4

Note Duncan's speech, lines 11-13. What quality does it show that Duncan lacked? Is this quality important to a king?

Why does Duncan now appoint his son to be Prince of Cumberland? Remember that in Scotland the crown did not always descend from father to son, but might go to any other member of the royal family.

What is the effect upon Macbeth of the naming of Malcolm Prince of Cumberland? Note carefully his aside. Of what is he thinking? Is he still determined to let things drift?

Scene 5

What traits of Macbeth's character are shown by Lady Macbeth's speech after she has read the letter? Is she eager for Macbeth to gain the crown?

What do you learn about herself from her words, "Come, you spirits," etc., lines 40-55. Would a woman naturally evil say this?

Her words in line 65 and following, "He that's coming," etc. show her quick to rise to a situation. What part does she say she will take in the affair that night?

Scene 6

Note how the calmness of this scene, the king's comments upon the pleasant situation of the castle, Banquo's remarks about the birds flocking around, are all in marked contrast to the tense emotion of the preceding scene.

Observe that Lady Macbeth is the only one to greet the king: why is not Macbeth there too? Note that Duncan asks, but Lady Macbeth does not reply.

Scene 7

Here again Macbeth reveals himself through soliloquy. A man planning to commit murder might be deterred by one of two reasons: fear that he will be found out and punished, or fear that he will suffer in another life for ill deeds done here. Which of these motives influences Macbeth?

When Lady Macbeth enters, what decision has Macbeth reached? At the end of the scene, what is he determined to do? What is the reason for his change of mind?

In real life, influences come to us from three spheres. The first is within ourselves; our desires, ambitions, dislikes, move us. The second sphere is that of people about us: we are moved by what they say or do. The third sphere is the supernatural: what we believe about this often governs or modifies our actions. From which of these three spheres is Macbeth influenced towards the killing of Duncan? At the close of this act, do we want to see Macbeth gain the crown?

Act II—Scene 1

What new character is introduced here?

How does this scene prepare us for a scene to come?

In Macbeth's soliloquy, is there an actual dagger which he sees? What do his words show about his state of mind?

Scene 2

Why had Lady Macbeth not committed the murder herself? What does this show about her?

Had Macbeth actually heard a voice as described in line 35? What does this speech show about him?

What is Macbeth's feelings as shown in the closing lines of the scene?

Scene 3

In the first part of this scene we have, in the grumbling of the drunken porter, one of the few touches of humor in this play. Observe that it comes between two scenes where emotion is keyed up to a high pitch: the scene of the murder, and the scene where the murder is discovered. The porter episode serves as a relief scene, to let down the tension for the moment.

In this scene we learn that Macbeth, going back to Duncan's room after the murder was discovered, had slain the two grooms. Was this as he and Lady Macbeth had planned? Does he admit in his explanation that the act was unwise? Is it the realization that Macbeth had blundered, coming on top of all that she had gone through, that makes Lady Macbeth faint?

Is there anything in the scene that shows that Malcolm and Donalbain already suspect Macbeth? In what words?

Scene 4

This scene shows us public opinion in Scotland. Is there anything that suggests that Macduff is not friendly to Macbeth?

At the end of this act, has Macbeth risen or fallen in our esteem, since Act I?

Act III—Scene 1

The opening lines show Banquo's thoughts. Does he suspect Macbeth of Duncan's murder? If so, why does he not speak out?

Note in the dialogue between Macbeth and Banquo how, by apparently careless remarks, Macbeth learns where Banquo and Fleance are to be that evening.

In the dialogue with the two murderers, notice how much pains Macbeth takes to convince the men that Banquo was their enemy. In a previous conversation, which he refers to here, he had worked with them to the same purpose. Do the men appear at all reluctant to carry out his orders? Why should he think they would require so much urging? Did he require it?

In this, Macbeth's second crime, did Lady Macbeth have any part? Does this indicate anything about Macbeth? What? Keep in mind as the play progresses to look for changes in character.

Scene 2

Note in this scene indications of how far Macbeth and Lady Macbeth are satisfied or happy, now that they have attained the throne. What do lines 4-6 tell us about Lady Macbeth's feelings?

What do lines 16-22 tell us about Macbeth? Does Macbeth confide to Lady Macbeth his intention to kill Banquo?

Scene 3

Some critics have held that the third murderer in this scene is Macbeth himself. But this supposition is not necessary. Macbeth had told the others that he would tell them later the exact time and place: the third murderer was sent to do this, and also, by adding a man, to make it more sure that Banquo and Fleance would fall.

Note that the escape of Fleance marks the first time that Macbeth's plans go wrong. Up to now everything has favored him: he won renown in battle, he was rewarded by the king with a title; Duncan's announced visit gave opportunity for the murder; the deed was accomplished, the flight of the king's sons put suspicion upon them, the crown was given to Macbeth,—everything has gone his way. But with the escape of Fleance comes the turn in his fortunes.

Scene 4

Here again we see fortune turning against Macbeth. The appearance of Banquo's ghost totally unnerves him; his wild speeches addressed to the ghost cannot help but arouse suspicions of his sanity in the minds of the guests, who see nothing to explain his conduct.

The question as to whether the ghost should be visible or not is one that has been much discussed. Certainly Macbeth sees the ghost, and unless it is visible to the audience, they cannot understand why Macbeth, when it vanishes, grows bold again, and when it reappears, he once more addresses it. That it should be seen by Macbeth and by the audience but not by the other guests is exactly parallel to the situation in Hamlet where, as he speaks to his mother, the ghost enters, and is seen by Hamlet and the audience, but not by the Queen.

Note in this scene preparation for the scene to follow: how is this done?

Scene 5

Here a new character is introduced, Hecate. She is not necessary to the story, and it has been conjectured that the whole scene was written by another person, probably after Shakespeare's death. It was a fairly common practice, then as now, to make changes in the text of a play during its production, and since Shakespeare's plays were not published until seven years after his death, we cannot say that we have them exactly as they were first written.

Scene 6

This scene serves to give us the state of public opinion in Scotland, showing that the lords are turning against Macbeth, and that he is suspected of the murder of Duncan and of Banquo.

This is another bit of evidence that Macbeth's fortunes are declining; he is losing the support of his nobles.

Act IV—Scene 1

This scene also divides itself into two parts. The first part, up to the entrance of Macbeth, prepares us for the second part: we learn more about the witches, and the horrible means they used to call up evil spirits to their aid. In these witch scenes, Shakespeare is following the beliefs of the time, as they are told in such books as Reginald Scot's *Discovery of Witchcraft*.

In the interview with the witches, Macbeth shows his old courage: he will see the masters of the witches, and he addresses them boldly. Note carefully the form each apparition has, and what it says, for these points are significant in later scenes.

The show of eight kings, followed by Banquo's ghost, is a prediction that eight descendants of Banquo will be kings.

In the conclusion of this scene, Macbeth suddenly determines upon his third crime. Does his wife have any part in this?

How do the concluding lines prepare for a scene to follow? Observe how closely the play is knit together by such means.

Scene 2

The opening lines of this scene, with the fear of Lady Macduff, and the warning of the messenger, serve to key up our feelings for what is to come.

The dialogue between Lady Macduff and her little son serves two purposes. By introducing a little humor, in the clever replies of the child, it eases the tension for a few moments. Again, by winning our sympathy for the child, it makes his death seem the more frightful, and so serves to turn us strongly against Macbeth. Just as Shakespeare in the first act of the play makes us want to see Macbeth succeed, so now he is making us want to see him overthrown.

Scene 3

This is a long and rather slow scene, the weakest in the play. It is interesting that in this scene Shakespeare follows the story in Holinshed's *Chronicle* very closely. Holinshed was no dramatist.

The passage where the English doctor enters and mention is made of touching for the King's evil, has of course no connection with the plot of the play. But King James of England, who was on the throne when this play was written, had revived the custom of touching for the evil, and it is probable that this passage was introduced to please the King.

Act V—Scene 1

This scene, one of the great scenes in the play, has no foundation in Holinshed. When Shakespeare depends entirely upon his own invention he is greatest.

What purpose is served by the conversation between the Doctor and the Gentlewoman, before the entrance of Lady Macbeth? The Gentlewoman refuses to repeat what Lady Macbeth had said: what effect has this upon the audience?

What different things does Lady Macbeth reveal in her speeches in this scene?

When she says, "The Thane of Fife had a wife: where is she now?" she refers to Lady Macduff. Why should this murder haunt her dreams? Had she any part in it?

Scene 2

This scene prepares us for the coming battle; it also shows the state of feeling in Scotland, towards Macbeth. His power is slipping from him.

Scene 3

Macbeth here appears in a half-frenzied condition. Just after he has protested that he will fear nothing, a servant enters, and at the sight of his pale face, Macbeth loses all control of himself and curses him: a most unkingly action.

Once more Macbeth reveals his deep discontent with life, in the lines beginning

"I have lived long enough."

Scene 4

Note that it is Malcolm who gives the order to cut off the branches at Birnam Wood and bear them to Dunsinane. Thus is fulfilled one prophecy, and the child crowned with the tree in his hand is seen to represent Malcolm.

What purpose does this scene serve?

Scene 5

Once more we see into the darkness of Macbeth's mind, in the lines beginning

"Tomorrow and tomorrow and tomorrow."

Read carefully lines 19-28. What do they tell us about Macbeth?

Why does Macbeth give the order to go out and attack when he had determined to stand a siege?

Scene 6

What is the purpose of this scene?

Note that it is Malcolm who directs the whole attack. Just as Shakespeare has, for several acts, been lowering Macbeth in our estimation, making us wish for his downfall, so now in several scenes he has been raising Malcolm in our opinion.

Scene 7

In this Macbeth shows a desperate courage; he still relies upon the witches' predictions. The closeness by which Macduff misses him in this scene rouses our interest for the encounter later.

Scene 8

The dialogue between Macduff and Macbeth serves to bring out the fulfillment of another prophecy: the bloody child is now seen to represent Macduff, for whose birth a surgical operation was necessary. Thus all the prophecies of the witches came true.

We have been desiring Macbeth's downfall for some time,

and it is only justice that Macduff should be the one to slay him. In this scene both these desires of ours are gratified. Further, in Malcolm's rewarding his followers we see another evidence of his fitness to become King of Scotland.

The Play as a Whole

The play ends, as Shakespeare's plays usually do, with a promise of a brighter future. Macbeth by his first crime has disturbed the moral orders; his ill-doing does not stop here, but crime follows crime, and the whole kingdom suffers from this man's acts. But retribution, though delayed, always comes. Even before Macbeth's defeat he has ceased to find any satisfaction in life, it seems to him "a tale told by an idiot, signifying nothing." Lady Macbeth, breaking at last under the terrific strain, takes her own life. Macbeth's defeat and death follow. So the crime has been atoned for, and with Malcolm's accession the moral order of the world once more asserts itself.

The play may be interpreted as showing the danger of ambition when totally unrestrained by moral or religious considerations. It shows, too, that when one attains his ambition by wrong means, he will find no happiness nor peace in his achievement.

Of the character of Macbeth, there are two possible views. One is, that he was rather a weak character, not naturally bad, but one who, influenced by supernatural powers, and driven on by his wife, was hurried into crime.

The other view holds that he was a strong character, very ambitious, and that even before he met the witches, he had thought of killing Duncan to gain the crown.

Which of these two views do you accept? Before answering, read carefully Act I, Scene 3, lines 135-42, and Scene 7, lines 47-54.

There are also two views of Lady Macbeth's character. According to one, she was as Malcolm describes her, a "fiend-like

Queen"; a woman of a bold, ambitious and cruel nature, who planned in cold blood to murder a guest under her own roof.

The other view is that she was ambitious for her husband rather than for herself; that she was not by nature cruel, but forced herself to act a cruel part, and that afterwards her remorse was so great that it draws her to madness and suicide.

Which of these views seems to you the true one? Before you decide, read her words in Act I, Scene 5 and Scene 7.

COMMENTS AND QUESTIONS

The Emperor Jones

Scene 1

The "antecedent action" in a play consists of the events which have happened before the beginning of the play and which the audience must understand in order to comprehend the play itself. In this scene the antecedent action is unfolded in a masterly manner.

1. Draw a plan of the stage setting and describe it in your own words.
2. What effect does the furtive conduct of the old negro woman have on the spectators?
3. Describe Smithers. What is a *cockney?*
4. What important fact does Smithers learn from the old woman?
5. Why does this knowledge give Smithers so much satisfaction?
6. Describe Jones—his personal appearance and bearing.
7. What do we learn about Smithers's activities on the island?
8. What was Jones's history before coming to the Island?
9. Explain the method by which he rose "from stowaway to Emperor in two years."
10. Explain the contrast between the status of the civilized American Negro and of the "bush" Negro which made this rise possible.
11. How have Jones and Smithers been mutually helpful in their trickeries?
12. Trace Jones's emotions upon learning that his followers have deserted him through the various stages of disbelief, indiffer-

ence, certainty, anger, boastfulness, and finally quiet confidence.

13. Why does the silver bullet give him confidence? How did the idea originate? Does he himself believe in its efficacy?

14. What preparations has he made for his escape?

15. What is a tom-tom? What was its significance to the natives? Why does it finally convince Jones that his career as Emperor is at an end?

16. Why is Smithers obliged to feel grudging admiration for Jones? Detail the instances in which he shows his admiration.

17. What disposal does the Emperor make of his property on the Island?

18. Describe how the Emperor manages to make his departure from his palace seem not like a rout.

Scene 2

1. Mention five details in the author's description of the stage setting which serve to make impressive the picture of gloom and "brooding, implacable silence."

2. What words of Jones at the beginning of the scene show that he still retains his confidence?

3. What words show that he still retains his high spirits?

4. What words reveal the very first hint of fear? (Note how from this point his fear steadily increases to the end of the play.)

5. What is the first blow to shake his confidence? Quote the words.

6. The "Little Formless Fears" are intended to be a sort of materialization of the vague, indefinite terror which has begun to take possession of Jones. Explain how this intention is made clearer by the statement that they are "striving to raise themselves on end," but "failing and sinking prone again."

7. How does Jones try to explain these uncanny forms?
8. Why does his revolver shot momentarily restore his confidence?
9. Why does it almost immediately thereafter add to his fears?

Scene 3

1. Describe the setting in your own words.
2. What did we learn about Jeff in Scene 1?
3. Can you think of a reason why Jeff, being a mere apparition, is made visible to the audience before he is to Jones?
4. With what two facts does Jones try to cheer himself up in the early part of the scene?
5. Are these efforts as successful as his efforts in the preceding scene?
6. Does Jones believe that Jeff is alive, or does he think it is a ghost? Give reasons.
7. Show that Jones's revolver shot had the same two effects on his mind as the shot in Scene 2.
8. What effect did the shot have, apparently, on the sound of the tom-tom?
9. How does the author make clear at the end of the scene that Jones's terror is rapidly increasing?

Scene 4

1. Explain how the setting differs from that of Scene 3.
2. Mention the details that show that Jones has lost most of his self-confidence and has become panicky.
3. What is the first hint that he is beginning to fall back upon religion in hope of safety? What had he said about religion in Scene 1?
4. How does he attempt to explain his seeing of the "ha'nts"? Does he really believe his own explanation?

5. What details in the author's description of the convicts indicate that they are apparitions?
6. Quote the lines from Scene 1 in which the incident herein reenacted is referred to.
7. Where in this scene does Jones show his greatest fear?
8. Where does he show the courage of desperation?
9. What effect does his revolver shot have this time?
10. How many bullets has he left?

Scene 5

1. Describe the setting.
2. What change is there in Jones's appearance?
3. Explain his further dependence on religion. Does it strengthen him?
4. Show that his native humor still emerges in spite of his terror.
5. Considering that the apparitions utter no words, explain how all the information can be given which the author indicates after the words, "The Auctioneer begins his spiel."
6. Compare this slave-auction scene with similar scenes you have read elsewhere. Does it recall an anecdote about Abraham Lincoln?
7. What is symbolized by the revolver shots which ended Scenes 2, 3, 4, 5?

Scene 6

1. Describe the setting.
2. Comment on Jones's hopelessness. Note that there is no longer even a suggestion of his old time confidence.
3. How has his personal appearance still further deteriorated?
4. Point out how the author's description makes clear that the apparitions in this scene are on a slave ship. Have you read any stories about slave ships?

5. Describe the effect which this sight has upon Jones.
6. How does this scene end?

Scene 7

1. Mention the details in the description of the setting which suggest that the scene is no longer in a forest in a West Indian island but in the heart of "darkest Africa."
2. Explain the significance of Jones's words: "I remember—seems like I been heah befo'."
3. Describe the Witch-Doctor.
4. Give in your own words the "narrative in pantomime" which is unfolded by the dance of the Witch-Doctor.
5. What does Jones understand that he is to do?
6. How does he save himself from the sacrifice?
7. Does the silver bullet fulfill the purpose for which it was intended?

Scene 8

1. Describe the setting.
2. Who is Lem?
3. Why is Smithers so contemptuous of the natives?
4. Why is Lem so confident that they will catch Jones?
5. How does Smithers explain Jones's presence in this part of the forest?
6. Where does Smithers show hatred of Jones?
7. Where does Smithers show a trace of his grudging admiration of Jones?
8. What is the significance of having Jones's death occur here in the edge of the forest—where his flight began?
9. Was Jones's prophecy concerning the silver bullet fulfilled? In the way Jones intended?
10. What is the author's purpose in having Smithers present at the beginning and again at the end of the play?

The Play as a Whole

1. Explain how the terrors of the vast forest and Jones's moral fear react on each other; how his fear is partly the cause, partly the result of these terrors.

2. Discuss the time element in the play. How much time elapses after each scene?

3. Note that in *The Emperor Jones* we have, as it were, only the last part of a play. In *Macbeth* the "turning-point" is in the middle of the play (Act III, Scene 3), while in this play it is at the end of Scene 1, when Jones begins his long flight. The events leading up to his becoming Emperor are suppressed, or casually alluded to in Scene 1. Suppose you were to extend this to a five-act play. The present Scene 1 would be in Act III. What would you put in Act I? Act II? Act IV? Act V?

4. Do the characters seem alive?

5. Why does Smithers feel himself inferior to Jones? Why does he admire him? Why does he hate him?

6. What admirable qualities has Jones? What despicable qualities?

7. Does the story seem probable or improbable?

8. Do the two dialects—cockney and Negro—add to or detract from your interest in the play?

9. Comment on the humorous touches in the play. Do they heighten the horror of the whole effect, or lessen it?

10. Make a study of the apparitions. Note that in Scene 2 they are "little formless fears," and in Scenes 3 and 4 they are reproductions of Jones's two murders. Look up in a good dictionary the meaning of the word "atavism," and continue with your study. In Scenes 5 and 6 Jones has gone back to the days of slavery; first he sees a slave auction, and then an earlier scene on a slave ship. In Scene 7 he is back amidst the savage superstitions of his remote ancestors. He has re-

verted to type. Has the author made his purpose clear and effective? Does Jones realize what he is experiencing? Is it natural that Jones's fears should produce this result? Have you read Vachel Lindsay's *The Congo*? If so, does it throw any light on this point?

QUESTIONS ON PLOT DEVELOPMENT

Macbeth

Act I—Planning the Murder

1. Discuss Macbeth's character as a warrior as described in Scene 2. Is there any hint that he is disloyal or ambitious fo. preferment? What does Duncan think of him?

2. Why does Macbeth start at the prophecies of the Witches? Might it indicate that he had secret ambition to become King? What else might it denote?

3. Where in Scene 3 does Macbeth admit to himself that the prophecy has put thoughts of murder in his heart?

4. Quote the words in Scene 3 with which he declares that he will take no steps toward becoming King.

5. Where in Scene 4 does he reveal that he is, nevertheless, thinking about it?

6. In Scene 5 in her soliloquy after reading Macbeth's letter, what does Lady Macbeth say about Macbeth's character?

7. What does she immediately think upon learning that Duncan is coming to the castle that evening?

8. How does she hint to Macbeth that she has planned the murder?

9. Why does Macbeth not reveal his own thoughts on the subject?

10. In his soliloquy in Scene 7 what are Macbeth's reasons against committing the murder? Do they sound convincing? What one valid reason against the murder does he not mention? Why?

11. With what words does Macbeth announce his decision against murder?

12. Explain how Lady Macbeth taunts, goads, and shames Macbeth into a decision in favor of the murder.
13. What are the details of the plan they agree upon?
14. In what words does Macbeth announce his final decision? How many times in this Act has he expressed an opinion? Quote the words of each. Does this vacillation show weakness on his part? Explain.

Act II—The Murder

1. What is the significance of the phantom dagger? What change takes place in its appearance during Macbeth's soliloquy?
2. At the beginning of Scene 2 how is Lady Macbeth's exaltation manifested? Her nervousness?
3. What is Macbeth's state of mind when he returns from committing the murder?
4. Detail six instances of Lady Macbeth's efforts to re-assure Macbeth.
5. Where in the scene does she rise to her greatest height of physical courage?
6. What different effect does the sound of the knocking have on Macbeth and on Lady Macbeth?
7. At what point in the scene is the emotional tension of the audience at the greatest? Explain.
8. Would the scene of the murder have been more effective if the actual stabbing had been shown on the stage? Give reasons.
9. How would you justify the introduction of the humorous porter's scene in the midst of the tragedy?
10. Do Macbeth and Lady Macbeth "carry off the situation" well when the dead body is discovered? How?

11. What deed of Macbeth is not according to the plans? What effect does it have on Lady Macbeth? Why?
12. Why do Malcolm and Donalbain decide to flee?

Act III—Conserving the Gains—Success and Failure

1. Does Banquo suspect Macbeth of the murder of Duncan?
2. Why does Macbeth fear Banquo?
3. Why does he resolve to kill him?
4. How does Macbeth make sure that the hired murderers will kill Banquo?
5. Show by quotation from Scene 2 that Macbeth and Lady Macbeth are not happy as King and Queen.
6. Why does Macbeth not tell Lady Macbeth of his plan to kill Banquo? What does this show as to the change in his character from what it was in Act I.
7. Was Macbeth the Third Murderer in Scene 3? Give reasons for and against.
8. Prove that Scene 3 is the turning-point of the play.
9. How does the news of the escape of Fleance affect Macbeth?
10. When the ghost is present at the banquet scene, do the guests know the cause of Macbeth's agitation? Does Lady Macbeth?
11. Should the ghost be visible to the audience, or should it be left to their imaginations? Give reasons.
12. What changes do you notice in Macbeth's character in Act III?
13. What are the people beginning to say about Macbeth and about Scotland's plight in Scene 6?

Act IV—Hastening to the Catastrophe

1. Describe the three apparitions and give the warning or prophecy of each.
2. In what ways is Macbeth falsely re-assured as to his future safety?

3. What news is brought that makes him resolve to take immediate action? What action?

4. What is revealed by this resolution as to the further degeneration of his character?

5. Is Macduff's escape to England a hint of the final downfall of Macbeth?

6. The escape of Macduff constitutes the second great failure in Macbeth's plans. What was the first?

7. Scene 3 clearly foreshadows Macbeth's downfall. Explain how it does this.

Act V—Retribution

1. What has been the cause of Lady Macbeth's physical and mental breakdown and death? Does her end satisfy "poetic justice"? Does it inspire pity? How does it affect Macbeth?

2. What do we learn about the morale of the avenging armies in Scenes 2, 4 and 6, and of Macbeth in Scenes 3 and 5? What does this make clear about the final outcome of the battle?

3. Quote the lines from Scene 5 and 8 in which Macbeth realizes that he has been duped by the Witches.

4. When the actual fighting begins, why does Macbeth seemingly recover his old courage? Does it gain your admiration?

5. Prove that Macbeth's violent death was the inevitable consequence of his crimes.

QUESTIONS ON CHARACTER STUDY

Macbeth

What do we learn about Macbeth from the opinions of the others in the play? What does the wounded officer say of him in Act I, Scene 2? What does Duncan say of him? What does Lady Macbeth say of him in Act I, Scene 5? What does Banquo say of him in Act III, Scene 1? Lennox, in Scene 6? Macduff, in Act IV, Scene 3?

What do we learn about him from his own actions? As reported by the wounded officer in Act I, Scene 2? When the Witches gave their prophecies in Scene 3? During the planning of the murder of Duncan? During the murder? After the discovery? Before the murder of Banquo in Act III, Scenes 1 and 2? During the banquet? On his visit to the Witches, Act IV, Scene 1? In the scenes before the battle in Act V? During the battle?

What do we learn about him from his own words? In the soliloquies: Act I, Scenes 3, 4, 7; Act II, Scene 1; Act III, Scene 1; Act V, Scene 8? Point out passages in the play wherein by his actions or his words he displays courage, duplicity, caution, foresight, cruelty, superstition, moral weakness, impetuosity.

Was he an opportunist? An egotist? A philosopher? A fatalist? A tyrant?

Was he a free moral agent? Was he a tool in the hands of fate? Was he dominated by Lady Macbeth?

Lady Macbeth

Was she selfishly ambitious? Was she mindful only of her husband? Was she cruel? Was she totally lacking in womanly tenderness? In moral sense? Was she vindictive? Domineering? Superstitious? Did she show any redeeming traits?

Where does she show insight into character? Quickness to grasp a situation? Physical courage? Physical weakness? Practicalness? Conscience?

Contrast Macbeth and Lady Macbeth before and after the murder of Duncan.

Banquo

In what way was the effect of the Witches' prophecies upon Banquo different from that upon Macbeth? What does this show as to Banquo's character? What mental trait do we infer from the fact that he tried to explain the phenomenon of the Witches? What moral trait, from the fact that he, unlike Macbeth, did nothing to hasten the fulfillment of the prophecies? Why did he have bad dreams? Was he of a trusting or a suspicious nature? What does Duncan say of him in Act I, Scene 4? Analyze Macbeth's estimate of his character in Act III, Scene 1. Is it correct?

Macduff

Prove that Macduff was honest, sincere, patriotic, self-sacrificing, courageous. Was he more of a man of action than thinker?

Jones

Where in the play does he manifest high spirits, egotism, arrogance, guile, courage, religious emotion, superstition, cowardice, his basic savagery? Is Jones a typical "primitive" man? Why?

GAME OF QUOTATIONS

I. See how many of the characters you can identify from the following quotations.
Who made the analysis? How far is it justified? Is it well done?

1.   'Tis much he dares,
   And, to that dauntless temper of his mind,
   He hath a wisdom that doth guide his valor
   To act in safety.

2. Your son, my lord, has paid a soldier's debt.
   He only lived but till he was a man;
   The which no sooner had his prowess confirmed
   In the unshrinking station where he fought,
   But like a man he died.

3. If I say sooth, I must report they were
   As cannons overcharged with double cracks.

4. My voice is in my sword, thou bloodier villain
   Than terms can give thee out!

5.   New honors come upon him,
   Like our strange garments, cleave not to their mold
   But with the aid of use.

6.   Not so sick, my lord,
   As she is troubled with thick-coming fancies,
   That keep her from her rest.

7.   I am one, my liege,
Whom the vile blows and buffets of the world
Have so incensed that I am reckless what
I do to spite the world.

8. Your face, my Thane, is as a book where men
May read strange matters.

9.   Art thou afeard
To be the same in thine own act and valor
As thou art in desire?

10.   There's no art
To find the mind's construction in the face;
He was a gentleman on whom I built
An absolute trust.

11. Some say he's mad; others, that lesser hate him,
Do call it valiant fury; but, for certain,
He cannot buckle his distempered cause
Within the belt of rule.

12.   But, for your husband,
He is noble, wise, judicious, and knows best
The fits o' the season.

13.   (Did you) know
That it was he in the times past which held you
So under fortune, which you thought had been
Our innocent self?

14.   Would thou hadst less deserved,
That the proportion both of thanks and payment
Might have been mine! Only I have left to say,
More is thy due than more than all can pay.

15. The earth hath bubbles as the water has,
    And these are of them.

II. *Each of the following expressions states a truth or what seemed
    like a truth to the one who said it. Can you identify the
    speaker? Will you analyze the value of the idea? Will you
    show how it applies to the scene in which it appears?*

1. And oftentimes, to win us to our harm,
   The instruments of darkness tell us truths,
   Win us with honest trifles, to betray 's
   In deepest consequence.

2. The attempt and not the deed confounds us.

3. The labor we delight in physics pain.

4. To show an unfelt sorrow is an office
   Which the false man does essay.

5. There's daggers in men's smiles.

6.   Nought's had, all's spent,
   Where our desire is got without content:
   'Tis safer to be that which we destroy
   Than by destruction dwell in doubtful joy.

7.   Things without all remedy
   Should be without regard: what's done is done.

8.   The feast is sold
   That is not often vouched, while 'tis a-making,
   'Tis given with welcome: to feed were best at home.

9. The flighty purpose never is o'ertook
   Unless the deed go with it.

10.　　　　When our actions do not,
　　　Our fears do make us traitors.

11.　　　　The king-becoming graces,
　　　As justice, verity, temperance, stableness,
　　　Bounty, perseverance, mercy, lowliness,
　　　Devotion, patience, courage, fortitude.

12. Things at the worst will cease, or else climb upward
　　　To what they were before.

13. The night is long that never finds the day.

14. Life 's but a walking shadow, a poor player
　　　That struts and frets his hour upon the stage
　　　And then is heard no more; it is a tale
　　　Told by an idiot, full of sound and fury,
　　　Signifying nothing.

15. Canst thou not minister to a mind diseased,
　　　Pluck from the memory a rooted sorrow,
　　　Raze out the written troubles of the brain
　　　And with some sweet oblivious antidote
　　　Cleanse the stuffed bosom of that perilous stuff
　　　Which weighs upon the heart?

COMPOSITION TOPICS

1. Tell the story of the rebellion against Duncan. Discuss the leaders Macdonwald and Cawdor, the allies from Ireland and Norway, Macbeth's prowess in battle, the result, the terms of capitulation, the fate of the leaders.
2. Elizabethan Witch Lore.
3. Portents and Omens in *Macbeth*.
4. The three apparitions—their prophecies and how they were fulfilled.
5. Macduff's choice—between his duty to his family and his duty to his country.
6. The three motives of Macbeth's career—his own ambition, the prophecies of the Witches, Lady Macbeth's urging. Evaluate them.
7. Contrast Macbeth and Banquo.
8. Contrast Macbeth and Macduff.
9. Contrast Banquo and Macduff.
10. Contrast Macbeth and Lady Macbeth.
11. The Sleep-walking Scene.
12. The most effective scene in the play.
13. Great actresses in the rôle of Lady Macbeth.
14. Destiny in the ancient Greek drama and in Macbeth.
15. How Macduff would tell the story.
16. Shakespeare's debt to Holinshed.
17. Macbeth—a great man, a great failure.
18. Ambition—right and wrong.
19. Macbeth's mistakes.
20. The secret of Jones's power over the natives.

21. Forest Terrors.
22. "Conscience makes cowards of us all."
23. Scenes from Jones's career as Pullman car porter.
24. The history of the Negro race as re-capitulated in Jones's visions.
25. Comparison of *The Emperor Jones* and Lindsay's *The Congo*.
26. African Witch lore.
27. Traits of Negro character exemplified in Jones.
28. O'Neill—dramatic innovator.
29. The opera *The Emperor Jones*.
30. Recent tendencies in American drama.

SHORT TYPE TESTS

I. True—False

Directions:—Copy on your paper the number of each question, and beside this number write T, if you think the statement true; F, if you think it false.

1. Jones wore patent leather shoes at the beginning of his flight.
2. In the convict scene Jones struck the Prison Guard with a shovel.
3. In Scene 5 Jones confessed that he had murdered Jeff.
4. Jones declared that Smithers had been in jail more than once.
5. Jones fired his silver bullet at the Auctioneer.
6. The sound of the tom-tom seemed louder at the end of Scene 6 than at the end of Scene 5.
7. Smithers believed in the efficacy of the silver bullet.
8. Lem was a former Pullman car porter.
9. The Witch-Doctor wore antelope horns.
10. Jones had hidden money under a white stone at the edge of the forest.
11. Ross remained loyal to Macbeth to the end.
12. Macbeth said, "More needs she the divine than the physician."
13. The final speech in *Macbeth* is uttered by Malcolm.
14. Lennox was present when the murder of Duncan was discovered.
15. In the banquet scene the guests saw the ghost of Banquo.
16. Lady Macbeth said that Duncan resembled her father.
17. Siward was a general in Macbeth's army.
18. Macbeth said, "Life is but a walking shadow."

19. Macbeth was the Thane of Glamis.
20. Macduff was the Thane of Fife.
21. Fleance became king after Macbeth's death.
22. Malcolm was older than Donalbain.
23. Macbeth's killing of Duncan's grooms was contrary to his original plans.
24. Macduff placed his duty to his family above his duty to his country.
25. Duncan suspected Macbeth of disloyalty.
26. There is no humor in *Macbeth*.
27. Lady Macbeth showed remorse of conscience.
28. Caithness was a Scottish nobleman.
29. Macbeth told Lady Macbeth of his plan to kill Banquo.
30. Shakespeare invented the entire plot of *Macbeth*.

II. Completion Test

Directions:—Copy on your paper the number of each question, and opposite each number write the facts that will complete the sentence truthfully.

1. Shakespeare got the material for his play from_____.
2. Two reasons why Macbeth feared Banquo were: (1)_____ _____ and (2) _____.
3. In the sleep-walking scene, Lady Macbeth revealed the murder of Lady Macduff when she said, "_____."
4. On the night of the murder the chamber next to Duncan's was occupied by_____.
5. Five Scottish noblemen were_____, _____, _____, _____, and _____.
6. Banquo told Fleance he did not wish to sleep because _____ _____.
7. Macbeth first resolved to kill Macduff after_____ _____.

8. Malcolm tested Macduff's loyalty by pretending that_____
   _____.

9. The turning point of the play is in the scene where_____
   _____.

10. Macbeth made sure that the murderers would kill Banquo by making them believe that_____.

11. Macbeth showed moral weakness when_____.

12. Macbeth showed physical courage when_____.

13. The murder of Duncan was discovered by_____.

14. Malcolm and Donalbain fled to England because they feared
    _____.

15. The suggestion to use the boughs of Birnam wood as camouflage was made by_____.

16. Macbeth was crowned King at_____.

17. Two of the leaders in the rebellion against Duncan were
    _____ and_____.

18. The rebels received help from Norway and_____.

19. The natives made bullets from_____.

20. The Witch-Doctor wore_____ and_____ around his neck and ankles.

21. The third apparition Jones saw was_____.

22. The tom-tom began with_____beats to the minute.

23. Smithers hated Jones because_____.

24. The first hint that Jones's flight through the forest would not be successful was given when at the edge of the forest he
    _____.

25. At the end of his flight Jones re-appeared at the edge of the forest because_____.

26. When Jones first saw the ghost of Jeff he thought_____.

27. Jones had planned that after his flight through the forest he would take refuge on_____.

28. Jones said that he learned the difference between "little stealin' and big stealin'" when he was_____.

29. Jones's first name was_____.
30. Jones's degradation was greater than Macbeth's because_____
_____.

III. Multiple-Choice Test

Directions:—Copy on your paper the number of each question and after each number write a, b, or c, choosing the one that you think most satisfactorily completes the statement.

1. *Macbeth* is written mainly in
       a. heroic couplets;
       b. prose;
       c. blank verse.
2. "Screw your courage to the sticking-place,
   And we'll not fail" was spoken by
       a. Lady Macbeth;
       b. Macbeth;
       c. Malcolm.
3. *Macbeth* contains
       a. no humor;
       b. one humorous scene;
       c. many humorous scenes.
4. Sweno was King of
       a. Norway;
       b. Ireland;
       c. England.
5. Banquo heard the prophecies of the witches with
       a. fear;
       b. curiosity;
       c. indifference.
6. In *Macbeth* the real conflict is between
       a. Macbeth and his conscience;
       b. Macbeth and Lady Macbeth;
       c. right and wrong.

7. Macbeth first began to lose faith in the witches' prophecies when
    a. Macduff escaped to England;
    b. Birnam Wood seemed to move;
    c. Lady Macbeth died.

8. Macbeth said he hesitated to kill Duncan because
    a. he feared the consequences;
    b. he had no opportunity;
    c. he knew it was wrong to take human life.

9. Banquo's ghost appeared
    a. once;
    b. twice;
    c. three times.

10. Macbeth's downfall began when
    a. Fleance escaped;
    b. Lady Macbeth died;
    c. Macduff fled to England.

11. Before the final battle Macbeth was
    a. calm;
    b. cautious;
    c. nervous.

12. The chief meaning of *Macbeth* is that
    a. revenge is sweet;
    b. evil is always punished;
    c. courage always prevails.

13. *The Emperor Jones* is written in
    a. heroic couplets;
    b. blank verse;
    c. prose.

14. The beats of the tom-tom during the play
    a. became ever faster;
    b. became ever slower;
    c. remained at the same rate.

15. Jones
> a. died of fright;
> b. killed himself with a silver bullet;
> c. was killed by the natives.

16. *The Emperor Jones* contains
> a. no humor;
> b. several humorous passages;
> c. very little humor.

17. Smithers admired Jones because
> a. he was successful in hoodwinking the natives;
> b. he was a fugitive from justice;
> c. he always seemed to have confidence in himself.

18. The environment of the Congo jungle in Scene 7 seemed familiar to Jones because
> a. he had been there before;
> b. it reminded him of home;
> c. he had reverted to savagery.

19. The beats of the tom-tom were first heard when Jones
> a. was talking to Smithers;
> b. struck a match in the forest;
> c. fired his revolver at Jeff.

20. Justice is satisfied in the play because
> a. Jones suffers from the terrors of the forest;
> b. the natives revenge themselves upon him;
> c. a silver bullet is the instrument of his death.

IV. Location Test

Directions:—Copy on your paper the number of each quotation. After each number write the name of the speaker, and briefly tell the circumstances under which the words were spoken.

1.   To be thus is nothing;
   But to be safely thus.

2. Thou art too like the spirit of Banquo; down!

3. To-morrow, and to-morrow, and to-morrow,
   Creeps in this petty pace from day to day.

4. Shake off this downy sleep, death's counterfeit,
   And look on death itself!

5. Good sir, why do you start, and seem to fear
   Things that do seem so fair?

6.   Nothing in his life
   Became him like the leaving it.

7. Ay, in the catalogue ye go for men.

8.   I will not yield,
   To kiss the ground before young Malcolm's feet.

9.   Present fears
   Are less than horrible imaginings.

10. Now good digestion wait on appetite,
    And health on both!

11. I have lived long enough: my way of life
    Is fallen into the sear, the yellow leaf.

12.   What beast was it then
    That made you break this enterprise to me?

13.   Fit to govern!
    No not to live!

14.   There's husbandry in heaven,
    Their candles are all out.

15.   The sleeping and the dead
    Are but pictures; 'tis the eye of childhood
    That fears a painted devil!

16.   Duncan is in his grave;
    After life's fitful fever he sleeps well.

17. Mine eyes are made the fools o' th' other senses,
    Or else worth all the rest.

PROJECTS

An unusual project was conducted by Mr. James P. Morris of the Hornell High School, Hornell, New York which is reprinted, as Project 1, with his permission.

Macbeth—"Not Guilty"

1. Having taught *Macbeth* after the usual fashion involving careful analysis and memorization of passages and the pointing of morals, I conceived the idea of conducting the trial of Macbeth, with the idea that it may be important for students to see something of good in every individual.

Primarily, the student must have the *actual* facts of the story correct. Next, we must presume a few things. These, in our case, were (1) Macbeth is on trial for the death of Duncan and the usurpation of his throne, (2) Lady Macbeth is on trial as an accomplice in the murder.

Dropping the actual facts in the play, we took the liberty of supposing that (1) Macbeth is taken in battle by Malcolm but is not killed, (2) that Lady Macbeth is alive, (3) that Banquo is attacked but not killed. The rest of the facts stand.

Upon the announcement that we were to have a trial, the class elected a judge, an attorney for the state, an attorney for the defense, and a jury. Parts were assigned the students as witnesses. We had a Banquo, a porter, of course, a doctor, gentlewoman, etc. Some student brought to class a few simple rules of courtroom procedure and the next day the trial began. The judge and two attorneys were good students; the others were average. Each student reviewed the play rather thoroughly and many quoted entire speeches of those with whom they came in contact in their discovery of Duncan in his chamber; the gentlewoman gave the entire sleep walking speech of Lady Macbeth in her testimony. The trial lasted two days and was interesting enough that in a class of 32 there was no occasion for checking on discipline at any time. On the third day the jury met and returned a verdict of "not guilty."

The importance? Orally, each one answered with logic and lacked the discomfiture accompanying oral topics; the play had been read rather thoroughly in looking for proof of every statement given in answer to the attorneys' questions; interest was remarkable; the poorest student in the class was excellent as the porter because he has a sense of humor and actually had learned all the circumstances attending his answering the gate. Allowing any student to hand a written suggestion to a witness gave everyone a chance to take part. The students were well pleased and as a class we rated the reputation, as the school paper said, of "disrupting three hundred years of literature." I need not suggest the interest adolescence attaches to revolution.

As for composition, I suggested that each member of the class, judges and all, consider himself a reporter at the trial. As for real journalism I merely mentioned that good news articles usually answered the questions who, when, why, where, what in the opening paragraph. The girls in the class wrote excellent human interest stories, which were better compositions, naturally, than were the news articles. The Variorum Edition of *Macbeth* was consulted to find out how Lady Macbeth was dressed. Many gave hints of the costumes of Sarah Bernhardt and Mrs. Siddons as Lady Macbeth, but they were elaborated upon and were made modern in description. Many told of Lady Macbeth's desire to help Macbeth, her ambition for him rather than herself, etc. Altogether, I had a set of themes which would have delighted the eye and egotism of any teacher. Some printed the entire article by hand on drawing paper, sketched in the likenesses of Macbeth and his lady, or gave the theme a screaming headline which was a composite of the headlines of the newspaper of the days previous to the trial. Two of the compositions found their way into the school journal, and an account of the trial was heralded in the local papers as well as in the journal of a metropolis 70 miles distant.

I can suggest no more profitable or interesting piece of project work than this. I shall never miss an occasion to experiment in the juvenile court where bright, interesting, healthy American boys and girls can review the facts of a great piece of literature, and proclaim the "dead butcher" not guilty.

2. Arrange a class presentation of the most effective scenes from *Macbeth* or *The Emperor Jones*. Costumes may be designed by the Art Department and made by the classes in sewing.

3. With the co-operation of the Manual Training Department or by the use of simple materials (soap box, cardboard, straw, etc.), construct an Elizabethan Theater. Assign one group to do the carpentry work, another to dress doll actors in appropriate costumes, etc.

4. Have members of the Art Department design stage sets for the various scenes. Effective sets may be made with the use of a shoe box, illustrations from the magazines, water color and oil paint.

5. Draw a floor plan of the Throne room in the *Emperor Jones; Inverness Castle.*

6. Organize a theater party for the next presentation of *Macbeth* in your community or the next showing of *The Emperor Jones* in the movies. Have the class write a critical review.

7. Compile a scrap book of post cards, pictures and materials relating to Shakespeare, the Elizabethan period or Stratford. These may be mounted on cardboard to make an effective poster for the class room or English office. If the school possesses a projector or stereopticon, the pictures might be thrown on the screen and accompanied by an interesting travelogue or lecture.

8. Produce a puppet show of *Macbeth* or *The Emperor Jones.* Jointed dolls or puppets can be easily designed, costumed, painted and manipulated by thread or wires.

EXAMINATION QUESTIONS

1. Assume that you have been asked to recommend to one of your friends a book which you feel certain he or she would enjoy. In a paragraph of about 150 words, explain why the book will interest your friend. You will need to describe briefly the kind of person your friend is, and to make clear one or at most two features of the book that will interest him or her, illustrating these features with specific material from the book.

Note: At some appropriate point in your paragraph, give the title of the book and the name of the author.

English Composition.

2. Among the headings under which books may be classified are the following:

(a) books which seek to bring to life a past age;
(b) books which deal with social problems;
(c) books which present familiar, everyday life;
(d) books which present a kind of life which is strange or remote.

(1) Choose a book you have read (novel, drama, biography) which seems to you to belong under *one* of these headings. Give its title, author, and classification [(a), (b), (c) or (d)].

(2) In a paragraph of about 150 words explain why you have classified the book under the heading you selected, and show, by describing a specific character or incident in the book, how your classification was appropriate. *English Composition.*

3. Since everyone has experiences which change in some impor-

tant way his opinions or attitudes, such experiences and their effects provide much material for novels, plays, and biographies.

There is a wide range of experiences of this sort: a change of environment, exposure to danger, the stimulus of new friends or new ideas, a serious illness, an encounter with misfortune. Whatever the experience may be, however, it will bring about, in the person who has it, changes in his opinions, attitudes, or understanding of the world in which he lives.

Select such an experience from the life of a character you know through your reading, or from your own life or from that of a friend. In a theme of from 400-600 words give an account of this experience and show its effects.

You will need to describe briefly the experience itself. Do not re-tell the whole plot of the story; avoid experiences which do not cause important changes. But your main problems are: to explain how the experience changed your chosen character's opinion, attitudes, or understanding, and to show by specific illustrations how these changes became evident.   *English Composition.*

4. Describe the part played in a novel or drama by some minor character.   *English Composition.*

5. Since novelists and dramatists endeavor to make the characters in their stories consistent, they often cause these characters to reveal, in different situations, the same trait of personality.

In a paragraph of 100-125 words show how one character in a novel or play reveals the same trait of personality in two different situations.   *English Composition.*

6. Choose some character who must make a decision, or solve a problem, which is important to him (or her). The character chosen may be yourself or some person with whom you are well acquainted, or may be taken from a biography, novel, play, or narrative poem you have read.

Write a theme of from 400-500 words about this character and the way in which he (or she) meets the situation. Your theme should be unified; it should contain brief statements of the problem confronting the character and the way in which that problem is met. Spend most of your time and space, however, on a discussion showing whether or not the character's decision and conduct are consistent with what he (or she) had previously said and done. If you take your character from a literary work do not attempt to summarize the whole story.

7. Compare a modern book with a classic of the same type, play with play, novel with novel, essay with essay, etc.
Restricted Examination

8. State four human problems that are the subjects of four plays that you have read. Give the title and author of each of these plays. Discuss the dramatic treatment of any two of these problems. *Comprehensive Examination, September*

9. Give titles and authors of four plays each of which involves one of the following elements: (a) jealousy; (b) the supernatural; (c) historical events; (d) mistaken identity; (e) filial duty; (f) buffoonery.

In the case of each of the four, state in one or two sentences which of the elements listed the play involves.

Discuss two of these four plays with specific reference to the elements you have chosen.
Comprehensive Examination, June

10. Choose a subject from the following suggestions and write on it a composition of about 300 words.

(a) a king in Shakespeare.
Comprehensive Examination

11. Show the conflict of impulses and reason in certain actions of *Hamlet* or *Macbeth*. *Restricted Examination*

12. With specific reference to either *Hamlet* or *Macbeth* show that Shakespeare used the soliloquy to reveal the secret motives or the state of mind of his principal characters.

Restricted Examination

13. A good novelist (or a good dramatist) makes the action of his plot seem natural. Write a composition on this topic.

Restricted Examination

14. To what extent was Duncan's character responsible for the course of events in Macbeth?   *Restricted Examination*

15. The reading and study of literature should help a student to know a good book when he sees one—to distinguish, for instance, between the temporary and the permanent, the false and the true.

With this statement in mind, discuss some of the elements or qualities which enable you to recognize a piece of literature as good. Illustrate your answer, giving titles and authors, with specific references to at least two works, selected from fiction, poetry or drama which you have read or studied.

Comprehensive Examination

16. Show that the violent deaths in *Hamlet* or in *Macbeth* do not constitute the tragedy of the play.

Restricted Examination

17. Justify the statement that Lady Macbeth has more genuine horror of crime than Macbeth.   *Restricted Examination*

18. "The novelist or dramatist cannot forego the charm of plot without losing a great and legitimate source of interest, but his plot ought not to be governed merely by external circumstances imposed upon the characters from without. It is rather deter- mined by the characters themselves; the outcome of those inner

impulses of human nature which it is the chief purpose of the novelist or dramatist to portray."

  (a) Illustrate the truth of this statement by the discussion of one novel and two dramas (one comedy and one tragedy). Answer as fully as your time permits.

  (b) Give titles and authors of two other novels or dramas in which you think external circumstances have an unusually important part. Give brief reasons for your choice.   *Comprehensive Examination*

19. One importance of the novel and the drama consists in the opportunity they afford to meet and appraise significant varieties of character and human experience.

Select from your reading (giving title and author) two novels and two plays. From each of these four works select and describe at some length an important figure who represents a significant type of human character.   *English*

20. Name *two* novels and *two* plays which you have read. Choosing each item from a different work, refer to (a) a character, (b) a setting, (c) a passage of prose or verse, (d) a climax, which impressed you, and tell why.

    English, September

21. What then are the sources of interest in literature? First, literature is our best means of finding out how, in any given historical period, men looked at facts, how they interpreted the world about them; second, literature best satisfies the love which all men have for good stories well told; third, literature is our best important source for a wide knowledge of the ideas and ideals which have influenced the world; fourth, literature is, for the average

man, the most accessible source of beauty; and fifth, literature is a never-ending delight to those who possess the craftsman's interest.

—Boas and Smith, *An Introduction to the Study of Literature.*
By permission of Harcourt, Brace & Co.

From novels, poems, dramas, biographies, or essays that you have read, select *three* works of considerable length, each of which has held for you a different one of these "sources of interest." Explain, with specific references to the contents of these books.

English, June

22. "This is no book; who touches this, touches a man."—Walt Whitman. Show how traits or characteristics of the authors are revealed in each of three novels or plays you have read.

23. *Directions:* Write a composition of about three hundred and fifty words, basing your discussion on the views expressed in the following quotation, and prefixing an appropriate title:

"When you think about Shakespeare, if you think about him at all and read him with an understanding heart, you come very close to the main cable of the high-tension currents of humanity."
—Christopher Morley.   *English, September*

Reprinted by special permission of the College Entrance Examination Board

NEW YORK STATE REGENTS EXAMINATIONS

1. In books, as in life, an incident that seems unimportant at the time of happening may lead to momentous results. From the novels and full-length plays you have read, choose any two selections. In each case show by definite references how a seemingly unimportant event led to either a happy or a tragic result. Give titles and authors. *English, Four Years, 1959.*

2. In reading, as in life, we may meet some people who are very wise and other people who are very unwise. From your reading of novels and full-length plays, choose a total of two books. For one book, show by definite references why you consider a person in the book to be very wise; for the other book, show by definite references why you consider a person to be very unwise. Give titles and authors. *English, Four Years, 1958.*

3. Often a scene in a novel or play is so dramatic that it might be effective if presented on radio or television. The scene may involve an exciting episode, a conflict between two persons, a surprise, or a happy or tragic incident. Choose two such scenes, one from a novel and one from a full-length play, and in each case show by specific references that the scene chosen would be effective on radio or television. Give titles and authors.
English, Four Years, 1957.

4. In literature we frequently meet persons who arouse our admiration or our dislike. Choose one person from a novel and another from a full-length play, and show by definite references why you admired one of these persons and disliked the other person. Give titles and authors. *English, Four Years, 1957.*

5. The possession of moral or spiritual values helps people to face the problems of living. The lack of such values often leads to unhappiness or tragedy. From the novels, full-length plays and full-length biographies you have read, choose two books, and in each case show by definite references how a person in the book was helped or hindered by the possession or lack of such values. Give titles and authors.   *English, Four Years, 1956.*

6. Answer *a* or *b*.

a. Many stories present the experience of young people. By references to a novel and a play, show to what degree the authors have presented young people as they really are. Give titles and authors.

b. In life a person may meet defeat (1) through another person, or (2) through a physical disability, or (3) through a serious weakness in his own mental or moral make up. Use a novel to show the truth of one of the above statements, and a play to show the truth of a second statement. Give titles and authors.

English, Four Years, 1955.

7. In literature, the minor characters sometimes interest readers as much as the leading characters. From two or more novels or full-length plays (using at least one book of each type), select four minor characters and show by definite references why each is interesting. Give titles and authors.   *English, Four Years, 1954.*

8. Some characters in novels and plays are definitely men or women of action; others are more inclined to be thoughtful or imaginative. Show by definite references that an important character in a novel or play belongs to the first group mentioned; in the same way justify placing a character from a different novel or play in the second group. Give titles and authors.

English, Four Years, 1954.